Stories of Success:

Mark the Match Boy
(Illustrated)

Stories of Success:

Mark the Match Boy
(Illustrated)

Horatio Alger, Jr.

Sumner Books
Hermosa Beach, CA

TABLE OF CONTENTS

A NOTE FROM THE PUBLISHER

Once crowned "America's most influential writer," Horatio Alger is hardly known today. Those who are familiar with him think "rags to riches," and that's about it. Most young people have never heard of him.

What an opportunity!

More than a hundred years before our contemporary self-help movement, Horatio Alger paved the way with his vivid illustrations of the keys to success and happiness. Today, Sumner Books is excited to introduce a new generation of Americans to some of the most inspirational stories ever written. Regardless of your age, you simply cannot read a Horatio Alger book without coming away with a good feeling.

Alger's books initially sold in the millions and then the tens of millions and finally the hundreds of millions. In fact, the Chicago Daily News once called Horatio Alger "America's best selling author of all time." Sumner Books is committed to bringing to life this best selling collection in the form of audiobooks read by professional actors and recorded with audio engineers in our studio. Our revised e-books, each with a detailed table of contents and colored illustrations, are professionally edited, including the occasional updating of phrases to make the books as easy to read today as they were when they were first published between 1865 and 1900.

Long after his death in 1899, the magazine Publishers Weekly wrote: "To call Horatio Alger Jr. America's most influential writer may seem like an overstatement ... but ... only Benjamin Franklin meant as much to the formation of the American popular mind."

Our goal is to bring back some of the influence that Alger exerted on millions of young people in America. Yes, it's retro; it's counterintuitive and totally contrary to the cynicism that has become a part of American culture. But we are proud to be leading a movement that is as positive and uplifting as the last pages of a Horatio Alger story.

Rick Newcombe
President
Sumner Books

Stories of Success

"Success is not measured by what you accomplish, but by the opposition you have encountered, and the courage with which you have maintained the struggle against overwhelming odds."
–Orison Swett Marden

CHAPTER I

RICHARD HUNTER AT HOME

"Fosdick," said Richard Hunter, "what was the name of the man who owed your father two thousand dollars, which he never paid him?"

"Hiram Bates," answered Fosdick in some surprise. "What made you think of him?"

"I thought I remembered the name. He moved out West, didn't he?"

"So I heard at the time."

"Do you happen to remember where? Out West is a very large place."

"I do not know exactly, but I think it was Milwaukee."

"Indeed!" exclaimed Richard Hunter, in visible excitement. "Well, Fosdick, why don't you try to get the debt paid?"

"Of what use would it be? How do I know he is living in Milwaukee now? If I should write him a letter, there isn't much chance of my ever getting an answer."

"Call and see him."

"What, go out to Milwaukee on such a wild-goose chase as that? I can't think what you are driving at, Dick."

"Then I'll tell you, Fosdick. Hiram Bates is now in New York."

"How do you know?" asked Fosdick with an expression of mingled amazement and incredulity.

"I'll show you."

Richard Hunter pointed to the list of hotel arrivals in the Evening Express which he held in his hand. Among the arrivals at the Astor House was the name of Hiram Bates from Milwaukee.

"If I am not mistaken," he said, "that is the name of your father's debtor."

"I don't know, but you are right," said Fosdick thoughtfully.

"He must be prosperous if he stops at a high-priced hotel like the Astor."

"Yes, I suppose so. How much good that money would have done my poor father," he added with a sigh.

"How much good it will do you, Fosdick."

Fosdick shook his head. "I would sell out my chance of getting it for ten dollars," he said.

—

3

"I would buy it at that price if I wanted to make money off you, but I don't. I advise you to attend to this matter at once."

"What can I do?" asked Fosdick, who seemed at a loss to understand his companion's meaning.

"There is only one thing to do," said Dick promptly. "Call on Mr. Bates this evening at the hotel. Tell him who you are, and hint that you should like the money."

"I haven't got your confidence, Dick. I shouldn't know how to go about it. Do you think it would do any good? He might think I was impertinent."

"Impertinent to ask payment of a just debt! I don't see it in that light. I think I shall have to go with you."

"I wish you would, that is, if you really think there is any use in going."

"You mustn't be bashful if you want to get on in the world, Fosdick. As long as there is a chance of getting even a part of it, I advise you to make the attempt."

"Well, Dick, I'll be guided by your advice."

"Two thousand dollars would be a pretty good windfall for you."

"That's true enough considering that I only get eight dollars week."

"I wish you got more."

"So do I, for one particular reason."

"What is that?"

"I don't feel satisfied to have you pay ten dollars a week towards our board while I pay only six."

"Didn't you promise not to say anything more about that?" said Dick reproachfully.

"But I can't help thinking about it. If we had stayed at our old boarding house on Bleecker Street, I could have paid my full share."

"But this is a nicer room."

"Much nicer. If I only paid my half, I should be glad of the chance."

"Well, I'll promise you one thing. If Mr. Bates pays you the two thousand dollars, you may pay your half of the expenses."

"Not much chance of that, Dick."

"We can tell better after calling at the Astor House. Get on your coat and we'll start."

—

While the boys, for the elder of the two is but eighteen, are making preparations to go out, a few explanations may be required by the reader. Those who have read "Ragged Dick" and "Fame and Fortune," the preceding volumes of this series, will understand that less than three years before Richard Hunter was an ignorant and ragged bootblack about the streets, and Fosdick, though possessing a better education, was in the same business. By a series of upward steps, partly due to good fortune but largely to his own determination to improve and to his hopeful energy, Dick had now become a bookkeeper in the establishment of Rockwell & Cooper on Pearl Street and possessed the confidence and good wishes of the firm in a high degree.

Fosdick was two years younger and, though an excellent boy, was less confident and not so well fitted as his friend to contend with the difficulties of life and to fight his way upward. He was employed in Henderson's hat and cap store on Broadway and was at present earning a salary of eight dollars a week. As the two paid sixteen dollars weekly for their board, Fosdick would have had nothing left if he had paid his full share. But Richard Hunter at first insisted on paying eleven dollars out of the sixteen, leaving his friend but five to pay. To this Fosdick would not agree and was with difficulty prevailed upon at last to allow Richard to pay ten; he has always felt a delicacy about this although he well knew how gladly his friend did it.

The room they now occupied was situated in St. Mark's Place which forms the eastern portion of Eighth Street. It was a front room on the third floor and was handsomely furnished. There was a thick carpet of tasteful appearance on the floor. Between the two front windows was a handsome bureau, surmounted by a large mirror. There was a comfortable sofa, chairs covered with hair-cloth, a center-table covered with books, crimson curtains, which gave a warm and cozy look to the room when lighted up in the evening, and all the accessories of a well-furnished room which is used at the same time as parlor and chamber. This, with an excellent table, afforded a very agreeable home to the boys, a home which, in those days, would cost considerably more, but for which, at the time of which I write, sixteen dollars was a fair price.

It may be thought that, considering how recently Richard Hunter had been a ragged bootblack content to sleep in boxes and sheltered doorways and live at the cheapest restaurants, he had become very luxurious in his tastes. Why did he not get a cheaper boarding place and save up the difference in price? No doubt this consideration will readily suggest itself to the minds of some of my young readers.

As Richard Hunter had a philosophy of his own on this subject, I may as well explain it here. He had observed that those young men, who out of economy contented themselves with small and cheerless rooms in which there was no provision for a fire, were driven in the evening to the streets, theaters, and hotels for the comfort which they could not find at home. Here they felt obliged to spend money to an extent of which they probably were not themselves fully aware, and in the end wasted considerably more than the two or three dollars a week extra which would have provided them with a comfortable home. But this was not all. In the roamings spent outside many laid the foundation of bad habits which eventually led to ruin or shortened their lives. They lost all the chances of improvement which they might have secured by study at home in the long winter evenings and which, in the end, might have qualified them for posts of higher responsibility and with a larger compensation.

Richard Hunter was ambitious. He wanted to rise to an honorable place in the community, and he meant to earn it by hard study. So Fosdick and he were in the habit of spending a portion every evening in improving reading or study. Occasionally he went to some place of amusement, but he enjoyed thoroughly the many evenings when, before a cheerful fire and with books in their hands, his roommate and himself added to their stock of knowledge. The boys had for over a year taken lessons in French and mathematics and were now able to read the French language with considerable ease.

"What's the use of moping every evening in your room?" asked a young clerk, who occupied a hall bedroom adjoining.

"I don't call it moping. I enjoy it," was the reply.

"You don't go to a place of amusement once a month."

"I go as often as I like."

"Well, you're a strange chap. You pay such a thundering price for board. You could go to the theater four times a week without it costing you any more, if you would take a room like mine."

"I know it, but I'd rather have a nice, comfortable room to come home to."

"Are you studying to become a college professor?" asked the other with a sneer.

"I don't know," said Dick good-humoredly, "but I'm open to proposals, as the oyster remarked. If you know any first-class institution that would like a dignified professor of extensive acquirements, just mention me, will you?"

So Richard Hunter kept on his way, indifferent to the criticisms which his conduct excited in the minds of young men of his own age. He looked farther than they and knew that if he wanted to succeed in life and win the respect of his fellow men, he must do something other than attend theaters and spend his evenings in billiard saloons. Fosdick, who was a quiet, studious boy, fully agreed with his friend in his views of life and, by his companionship, did much to strengthen and confirm Richard in his resolution. He was less ambitious than Dick and perhaps loved study more for its own sake.

With these explanations we shall now be able to start fairly in our story.

CHAPTER II

AT THE ASTOR HOUSE

The two friends started from their room about seven o'clock and walked up to Third Avenue where they jumped on board a horse car and within half an hour were landed at the foot of the City Hall Park, opposite Beekman Street. From this point it was necessary only to cross the street to the Astor House.

The Astor house is a massive pile of gray stone and has a solid look, as if it might stand for hundreds of years. When it was first erected, a little more than thirty years ago, it was considered far uptown, but now it is far downtown, so rapid has been the growth of the city.

Richard Hunter ascended the stone steps with a firm step, but Henry Fosdick lingered behind.

"Do you think we had better go up, Dick?" he asked irresolutely.

"Why not?"

"I feel awkward about it."

"There is no reason why you should. The money belongs to you rightfully as the representative of your father, and it is worth trying for."

"I suppose you are right, but I shan't know what to say."

"I'll help you along if I find you need it. Come along."

Those who possess energy and a strong will generally gain their point, and it was so with Richard Hunter. They entered the hotel and, ascending some stone steps, found themselves on the main floor where the reading room, clerk's office and dining room are located.

Dick, to adopt the familiar by which his companion addressed him, stepped up to the desk and drew towards him the book of arrivals. After a brief search he found the name of "Hiram Bates, Milwaukee, Wis.," toward the top of the left-hand page.

"Is Mr. Bates in?" he inquired of the clerk, pointing to the name.

"I will send and inquire, if you will write your name on this card."

Dick thought it would be best to send his own name, as that of Fosdick might lead Mr. Bates to guess the business on which they had come.

He accordingly wrote his name, Richard Hunter, in his handsomest handwriting and handed it to the clerk.

That functionary touched a bell. The summons was answered by a servant.

"James, go to No. 147, and see if Mr. Bates is in. If he is, give him this card."

The messenger departed at once and returned quickly.

"The gentleman is in and would be glad to have Mr. Hunter walk up."

"Come along, Fosdick," said Dick in a low voice.

Fosdick obeyed, feeling very nervous. Following the servant upstairs, they soon stood before No. 147.

James knocked.

"Come in," was heard from inside, and the two friends entered.

They found themselves in a comfortable furnished room. A man of fifty-five, rather stout in build and with iron-gray hair, rose from his chair before the fire and looked rather inquiringly. He seemed rather surprised to find that there were two visitors as well as at the evident youth of both.

"Mr. Hunter?" he said inquiringly, looking from one to the other.

"That is my name," said Dick promptly.

"Have I met you before? If so, my memory is at fault."

"No, sir, we have never met."

"I presume you have business with me. Be seated, if you please."

"First," said Dick, "let me introduce Henry Fosdick."

"Fosdick!" repeated Hiram Bates, with a slight tinge of color.

"I think you knew my father," said Fosdick nervously.

"Your father was a printer, was he not?" inquired Mr. Bates.

"Yes, sir."

"I do remember him. Do you come from him?"

Fosdick shook his head.

"He has been dead for two years," he said sadly.

"Dead!" repeated Hiram Bates, as if shocked. "Indeed I am sorry to hear it."

He spoke with evident regret, and Henry Fosdick, whose feelings toward his father's debtor had not been very friendly, noticed this and was softened by it.

"Did he die in poverty, may I ask?" inquired Mr. Bates after a pause.

"He was poor," said Fosdick. "That is, he had nothing laid-up, but his wages were enough to support him and myself comfortably."

"Did he have any other family?"

"No, sir. My mother died six years ago, and I had no brothers or sisters."

"He left no property then?"

"No, sir."

"Then I suppose he was able to make no provision for you?"

"No, sir."

"But you probably had some relatives who came forward and provided for you?"

"No, sir. I had no relatives in New York."

"What, then, did you do? Excuse my questions, but I have a motive in asking."

"My father died suddenly, having fallen from a Brooklyn ferryboat and drowned. He left nothing, and I knew of nothing better to do than to go into the streets as a bootblack."

"Surely you are not in that business now?" said Mr. Bates, glancing at Fosdick's neat appearance.

Mr. Hiram Bates, now living in Milwaukee, Wisconsin.

"No, sir. I was fortunate enough to find a friend," here Fosdick glanced at Dick, "who helped me along and encouraged me to apply for a job in a Broadway store. I have been there for a year and a half."

"What wages do you get? Excuse my curiosity, but your story interests me."

"Eight dollars a week."

"And do you find you can live comfortably on that?"

"Yes, sir. That is, with the assistance of my friend here."

"I am glad you have a friend who is able and willing to help you."

"It is not worth mentioning," said Dick modestly. "I have received as much help from him as he has from me."

"I see at any rate that you are good friends, and a good friend is worth having. May I ask, Mr. Fosdick, whether you ever heard your father refer to me in any way?"

"Yes, sir."

"You are aware, then, that there were some money arrangements between us?"

"I have heard him say that you had two thousand dollars of his but that you failed and that it was lost."

"He informed you rightly. I will tell you the particulars, if you are not already aware of them."

"I should be very glad to hear them, sir. My father died so suddenly that I never knew anything more than that you owed him two thousand dollars."

"Five years ago," commenced Mr. Bates, "I was a broker in Wall Street. As for my business, I was expected to know the best investments. Some persons brought me money to keep for them, and I either agreed to pay them a certain rate of interest or gave them an interest in my speculations. Among the persons was your father. The way in which I got acquainted with him was this: having occasion to get some prospectuses of a new company printed, I went to the office with which he was connected. There was some error in the printing, and he was sent to my office to speak with me about it. When our business was concluded, he waited a moment and then said, 'Mr. Bates, I have saved up two thousand dollars in the last ten years, but I don't know much about investments, and I should consider it a favor if you would advise me.'

"'I will do so with pleasure,' I said. 'If you desire it I will take charge of it for you and either allow you six percent interest or give you a share from the profits I may make from investing it.'

"Your father said that he should be glad to have me take the money for him, but he would prefer regular interest to uncertain profits. The next day he brought the money and put it in my hands. To confess the truth I was glad to have him do so for I was engaged in extensive speculations and thought I could make use of it to my advantage. For a year I paid him the interest regularly. Then there came a great catastrophe, and I found my brilliant speculations were but bubbles which broke and left me but a mere pittance instead of the hundred thousand dollars which I considered myself worth. Of course those who had placed money in my hands suffered, and among them was your father. I confess that I regretted his loss as much as that of any one, for I liked his straightforward manner and was touched by his evident confidence in me."

Mr. Bates paused a moment and then resumed.

"I left New York and went to Milwaukee. Here I was obliged to begin life anew, or nearly so, for I only carried a thousand dollars with me. But I have greatly prospered since then. I took warning by my past failures and have succeeded, by care and good fortune, in accumulating nearly as large a fortune as the one of which I once thought myself possessed. When fortune began to smile upon me I thought of your father and tried through an agent to find him. But he reported to me that his name was not to be found either in the New York or Brooklyn directory, and I was too busily engaged to come myself and make inquiries. But I am glad to find that his son is living and that I yet have it in my power to make restitution."

Fosdick could hardly believe his ears. Was he after all to receive the money, which he had supposed irrevocably lost?

As for Dick, it is not too much to say that he felt even more pleased at the prospective good fortune of his friend than if it had fallen to himself.

CHAPTER III

FOSDICK'S FORTUNE

Mr. Bates took from his pocket a memorandum book and jotted down a few figures in it.

"As nearly as I can remember," he said, "it is four years since I ceased paying interest on the money which your father entrusted to me. The rate I agreed to pay was six percent. How much will that amount to?"

"Principal and interest come to two thousand four hundred and eighty dollars," said Dick promptly.

Fosdick's breath was almost taken away as he heard this sum mentioned. Could it be possible that Mr. Bates intended to pay him as much as this? Why, it would be a fortune.

"Your figures would be quite correct, Mr. Hunter," said Mr. Bates, "but for one consideration. You forget that your friend is entitled to compounded interest as no interest has been paid for four years. Now, as you are no doubt used to figures, I will leave you to make the necessary correction."

Mr. Bates tore a leaf from his memorandum book as he spoke and handed it with a pencil to Richard Hunter.

Dick made a rapid calculation and reported two thousand five hundred and twenty-four dollars.

"I seems then, Mr. Fosdick," said Mr. Bates, "that I am your debtor to a very considerable amount."

"You are very kind, sir," said Fosdick, "but I shall be quite satisfied with the two thousand dollars without any interest."

"Thank you for offering to relinquish the interest, but it is only right that I should pay it. I have had the use of the money, and I certainly would not wish to defraud you out of a penny of the sum which it took your father ten years of industry to accumulate. I wish he were living now to see justice done to his son."

"So do I," said Fosdick earnestly. "I beg your pardon, sir," he said after a moment's pause.

"Why?" asked Mr. Bates in a tone of surprise.

"Because," said Fosdick, "I have done you injustice. I thought you failed in order to make money and intended to cheat my father out of his savings. That made me feel bitter towards you."

"You were justified in feeling so," said Mr. Bates. "Such cases are so common that I am not surprised at your opinion of me. I ought to have explained my position to your father and promised to make restitution whenever it should be in my power. But at the time I was discouraged and could not foresee the favorable turn which my affairs have since taken. Now," he added with a change of voice, "we will arrange about the payment of this money."

"Do not pay it until it is convenient, Mr. Bates," said Fosdick.

"Your proposal is kind but scarcely business-like, Mr. Fosdick," said Mr. Bates. "Fortunately it will occasion me no inconvenience to pay you at once. I have not the money with me as you may suppose, but I will give you a check for the amount upon the Broadway Bank with which I have an account, and it will be duly honored on the presentation tomorrow. You may in return make out a receipt in full for the debt and interest. Wait a moment. I will ring for writing materials."

These were soon brought by a servant of the hotel, and Mr. Bates filled in a check for the sum specified above while Fosdick, scarcely knowing whether he was awake or dreaming, made out a receipt to which he attached his name.

"Now," said Mr. Bates, "we will exchange documents."

Fosdick took the check and deposited it carefully in his pocketbook.

"It is possible that payment might be refused to a boy like you, especially as the amount is so large. At what time will you be disengaged tomorrow?"

"I am absent from the store from twelve to one for lunch."

"Very well. Come to the hotel as soon as you are free, and I will accompany you to the bank and get the money for you. I advise you, however, to leave it there on deposit until you have a chance to invest it."

"How would you advise me to invest it, sir?" asked Fosdick.

"Perhaps you cannot do better than buy shares of some good bank. You will then have no care except to collect your dividends twice a year."

"That is what I should like to do," said Fosdick. "What bank would you advise?"

"The Broadway Bank or Bank of Commerce are both good banks. I will attend to the matter for you if you desire it."

"I should be very glad if you would, sir."

14

"Then that matter is settled," said Mr. Bates. "I wish I could as easily settle another matter which has brought me to New York at this time and which, I confess, occasions me considerable perplexity."

The boys remained respectfully silent, though not without curiosity as to what this matter might be.

Mr. Bates seemed plunged in thought for a short time. Then, speaking as if to himself, he said in a low voice, "Why should I not tell them? Perhaps they may help me."

"I believe," he said, "I will take you into my confidence. You may be able to render me some assistance in my perplexing business."

"I shall be very glad to help you if I can," said Dick.

"And I also," said Fosdick.

"I have come to New York in search of my grandson," said Mr. Bates.

"Did he run away from home?" asked Dick.

"No, he has never lived with me. Indeed, I may add that I have never seen him since he was an infant."

The boys looked surprised.

"How old is he now?" said Fosdick.

"He must be about ten years old. But I see that I must give you the whole story of what is a painful passage in my life, or you will be in no position to help me.

"You must know then that twelve years ago I considered myself rich and lived in a handsome house uptown. My wife was dead, but I had an only daughter who I believe was generally considered attractive, if not beautiful. I had set my heart upon her making an advantageous marriage, that is marrying a man of wealth and social position. I had in my employ a clerk of excellent business abilities and of good personal appearance whom I sometimes invited to my house when I entertained company. His name was John Talbot. I never suspected that there was any danger of my daughter falling in love with the young man until one day he came to me and overwhelmed me with surprise by asking for her hand in marriage.

"You can imagine that I was very angry, whether justly or not I will not pretend to say. I dismissed the young man from my employ and informed him that never, under any circumstances, would I consent to his marrying Irene. He was a high-spirited young man, and though he did not answer me, I saw by the expression of his face that he meant to persevere in his suit.

"A week later my daughter was missing. She left behind a letter stating that she could not give up John Talbot and that by the time I read the letter she would be his wife. Two days later a Philadelphia paper was sent to me containing a printed notice of their marriage, and the same mail brought me a joint letter from both asking for my forgiveness.

"I had no objections to John Talbot except his poverty, but my ambitious hopes were disappointed, and I felt the blow severely. I returned the letter to the address given, accompanied by a brief line to Irene to the effect that I disowned her and would never more acknowledge her as my daughter.

"I saw her only once after that. Two years after, she appeared suddenly in my library, having been admitted by the servant, with a child in her arms. But I had hardened my heart against her, and though she besought my forgiveness, I refused it and requested her to leave the house. I cannot forgive myself when I think of my unfeeling severity. But it is too late to redeem the past. As far as I can, I would like to atone for it.

"A month ago I heard that both Irene and her husband were dead, the latter five years ago, but that the child, a boy, is still living, probably in deep poverty. He is my only descendant, and I seek to find him, hoping that he may be a joy and solace to me in my old age which will soon be upon me. It is for the purpose of tracing him that I have come to New York. When you," turning to Fosdick, "referred to your being compelled to resort to the streets and the hard life of a bootblack, the thought came to me that my grandson may be reduced to a similar extremity. It would be hard indeed that he should grow up ignorant, neglected, and subject to every privation when a comfortable and even luxurious home awaits him can only be found."

"What is his name?" inquired Dick.

"My impression is that he was named after his father, John Talbot. Indeed, I am quite sure that my daughter wrote me to this effect in a letter which I returned after reading."

"He is about ten years old?"

"I used to know most of the bootblacks and newsboys when I was in the business," said Dick reflectively, "but I cannot recall that name."

"Were you ever in the business, Mr. Hunter," asked Mr. Bates in surprise.

"Yes," said Richard Hunter smiling. "I used to be one of the most ragged bootblacks in the city. Don't you remember my Washington coat and Napoleon pants, Fosdick?"

"Surely that was many years ago?"

"I remember them well."

"It is not yet two years since I gave up blacking boots."

"You surprise me Mr. Hunter," said Mr. Bates. "I congratulate you on your advance in life. Such a rise shows remarkable energy on your part."

"I was lucky," said Dick modestly. "I found some good friends who helped me along. But about your grandson. I have quite a number of friends among the street boys, and I can inquire of them whether any boy named John Talbot has joined their ranks since my time."

"I shall be greatly obliged to you if you will," said Mr. Bates. "But it is quite possible that circumstances may have led to a change of name so that it will not do to trust too much to this. Even if no boy bearing that name is found, I shall feel that there is this possibility in my favor."

"That is true," said Dick. "It is very common for boys to change their name. Some can't remember whether they ever had any names and pick out one to suit themselves or perhaps get one from those they go with. There was one boy I knew named 'Horace Greeley.' Then there were 'Fat Jack,' 'Pickle Nose,' 'Cranky Jim,' 'Tickle-me-Foot,' and plenty of others.* You knew some of them, didn't you, Fosdick?"

"I knew 'Fat Jack' and 'Tickle-me-Foot,'" answered Fosdick.

"This increases the difficulty of finding and identifying the boy," said Mr. Bates. "Here," he said, taking a card photograph from his pocket, "is a picture of my daughter at the time of her marriage. I have had these taken from a portrait in my possession."

"Can you spare me one?" asked Dick. "It may help me to find the boy."

"I will give one to each of you. I need not say that I shall feel most grateful for any service you may be able to render me and will gladly reimburse any expenses you may incur, besides paying you liberally for your time. It will be better perhaps for me to leave fifty dollars with each of you to defray any expenses you may have."

"Thank you," said Dick, "but I am well supplied with money and will advance whatever is needful, and if I succeed I will hand in my bill."

Fosdick expressed himself in a similar way, and after some further conversation, he and Dick rose to go.

"I congratulate you on your wealth, Fosdick," said Dick when they were outside. "You're richer than I am now."

"I never should have got this money but for you, Dick. I wish you'd take some of it."

"Well, I will. You may pay my fare home on the horse cars."

"But really I wish you would."

But this Dick positively refused to do, as might have been expected. He was himself the owner of two uptown lots which he eventually sold for five thousand dollars, though they only cost him one, and he had three hundred dollars in the bank. He agreed, however, to let Fosdick henceforth bear his share of the expenses of board, and this added two dollars a week to the sum he was able to lay up.

CHAPTER IV

A DIFFICULT POSITION

It need hardly be said that Fosdick was punctual to his appointment at the Astor House on the following day.

He found Mr. Bates in the reading room looking over a Milwaukee paper.

"Good morning, Mr. Fosdick," he said, extending his hand. "I suppose your time is limited, therefore it will be best for us to go at once to the bank."

"You are very kind, sir, to take so much trouble on my account," said Fosdick.

"We ought all to help each other," said Mr. Bates. "I believe in that doctrine, though I have not always lived up to it. On second thoughts," he added as they got out in front of the hotel, "if you approve of my suggestions about the purchase of bank shares, it may not be necessary to go to the bank, as you can take this check in payment."

"Just as you think best, sir. I can depend upon your judgement as you know much more of such things than I."

"Then we will go at once to the office of Mr. Ferguson, a Wall Street broker and an old friend of mine. There we will give an order for some bank shares."

Together the two walked down Broadway until they reached Trinity Church, which fronts the entrance to Wall Street. Here then they crossed the street and soon reached the office of Mr. Ferguson.

Mr. Ferguson, a pleasant-looking man with sandy hair and whiskers, came forward and shook Mr. Bates cordially by the hand.

"Glad to see you, Mr. Bates," he said. "Where have you been for the last four years?"

"In Milwaukee. I see you are at the old place."

"Yes, plodding along as usual. How do you like the West?"

"I have found it a good place for business, though I am not sure whether I like it as well to live in as New York."

"Shan't you come back to New York some time?"

Mr. Bates shook his head.

"My business ties me to Milwaukee," he said. "I doubt if I shall ever return."

"Who is this young man?" said the broker looking at Fosdick. "He is not a son of yours, I think?"

"No. I am not fortunate enough to have a son. He is a young friend who wants a little business done in your line, and I have accordingly brought him to you."

"We will do our best for him. What is it?"

"He wants to purchase twenty shares in some good city bank. I used to know all about such matters when I lived in the city, but I am out of the way of such knowledge now."

"Twenty shares, you said?"

"Yes."

"It happens quite oddly that a party brought in only fifteen minutes ago twenty shares in the National Bank to dispose of. It is a good bank, and I don't know that he can do any better than to take them."

"Yes, it is a good bank. What interest does it pay now?"

"Eight percent."

"That is good. What is the market value of the stock?"

"It is selling this morning at one hundred and twenty."

"Twenty shares then will amount to twenty-four hundred dollars."

"Precisely."

This was before the war. Now most of the National Banks in New York pay ten percent, some even higher.

"Well, perhaps we had better take them. What do you say, Mr. Fosdick?"

"If you advise it, sir, I shall be very glad to do so."

"Then the business can be accomplished at once, as the party left us his signature authorizing the transfer."

The transfer was rapidly effected. The broker's commission of twenty-five cents per share amounted to five dollars. It was found on paying this, added to the purchase money, that one hundred and nineteen dollars remained, the check being for two thousand five hundred and twenty-four dollars.

The broker took the check and returned this sum, which Mr. Bates handed to Fosdick.

"You may need this for a reserve fund," he said, "to draw upon if needful until your dividend comes due. The bank shares will pay you probably one and sixty dollars per year."

"One hundred and sixty dollars!" repeated Fosdick in surprise. "That is little more than three dollars a week."

"Yes."

"It will be very acceptable as my salary at the store is not enough to pay my expenses."

"I would advise you not to break in upon your capital if you can avoid it," said Mr. Bates. "By and by, if your salary increases, you may be able to add the interest yearly to the principal so that it may be accumulating till you are a man when you may find it of use in setting you up in business."

"Yes, sir. I will remember that. But I can hardly realize that I am really the owner of twenty bank shares."

"No doubt it seems sudden to you. Don't let it make you extravagant. Most boys of your age would need a guardian, but you have had so much experience in taking care of yourself that I think you can get along without one."

"I have my friend Dick to advise me," said Fosdick.

"Mr. Hunter seems quite a remarkable young man," said Mr. Bates. "I can hardly believe that his past history has been as he gave it."

"It is strictly true, sir. Three years ago he could not read or write."

"If he continues to display the same energy, I can predict for him a prominent position in the future."

"I am glad to hear you say so, sir. Dick is a very good friend of mine."

"Now, Mr. Fosdick, it is time you were thinking of lunch. I believe this is your lunch hour?"

"Yes, sir."

"And it is nearly over. You must be my guest today. I know of a quiet little lunch room nearby which I used to frequent some years ago when I was in business on this street. We will drop in there, and I think you will be able to get through in time."

Fosdick could not well decline the invitation, but accompanied Mr. Bates to the place referred to where he had a better meal than he was accustomed to. It was finished in time, for as the clock on the city hall struck one, he reached the door of Henderson's store.

Fosdick could not very well banish from his mind the thoughts of his extraordinary change of fortune, and I am obliged to confess that he did not discharge his duties quite as faithfully as usual that afternoon. I will mention one rather amusing instance of his preoccupation of mind.

A lady entered the store, leading by the hand her son Edwin, a little boy of seven.

"Have you any hats that will fit my little boy?" she said.

"Yes, ma'am," said Fosdick absently, and he brought forward a large-sized man's hat of the kind popularly known as "stove-pipe."

"How will this do?" asked Fosdick.

"I don't want to wear such an ugly hat as that," said Edwin in dismay.

The lady looked at Fosdick as if she had very strong doubts of his sanity. He saw his mistake and, coloring deeply, said in a hurried tone, "Excuse me, I was thinking of something else."

The next selection proved more satisfactory, and Edwin went out of the store feeling quite proud of his new hat.

Towards the close of the afternoon, Fosdick was surprised at the entrance of Mr. Bates. He came up to the counter where he was standing and said, "I am glad I have found you in. I was not quite sure if this was the place where you were employed."

"I am glad to see you, sir," said Fosdick.

"I have just received a telegram from Milwaukee," said Mr. Bates, "summoning me home immediately on matters connected with business. I shall not therefore be able to remain here to follow up the search upon which I had entered. As you and your friend have kindly offered your assistance, I am going to leave the matter in your hands and will authorise you to incur any expenses you may deem advisable, and I will gladly reimburse you whether you succeed or not."

Fosdick assured him that they would spare no efforts, and Mr. Bates, after briefly thanking him and giving him his address, hurried away, as he had determined to start on his return home that very night.

CHAPTER V

INTRODUCES MARK THE

MATCH BOY

It was growing dark -- though yet scarcely six o'clock, for the day was one of the shortest in the year -- when a small boy, thinly clad, turned down Frankfort Street on the corner opposite French's Hotel. He had come up Nassau Street, passing the Tribune office and the old Tammany Hall, now superseded by the substantial new Sun building.

He had a box of matches under his arm of which very few seemed to have been sold. He had a weary, spiritless air and walked as if quite tired. He had been on his feet all day and was faint with hunger, having eaten nothing but an apple to sustain his strength. The thought that he was near his journey's end did not seem to cheer him much. Why this should be so will speedily appear.

He crossed William Street, passed Gold Street, and turned down Vandewater Street leading out of Frankfort's Street on the left. It is in the form of a short curve, connecting with the most crooked of all New York Avenues, Pearl Street. He paused in front of a shabby house and went upstairs. The door of a room on the third floor was standing ajar. He pushed it open and entered, not without a kind of shrinking.

A coarse-looking woman was seated before a scanty fire. She had just thrust a bottle into her pocket after taking a copious draught therefrom, and her flushed face showed that this had long been a habit with her.

"Well, Mark, what luck tonight?" she said in a husky voice.

"I didn't sell much," said the boy.

"Didn't sell much? Come here," said the woman sharply.

Mark came up to her side, and she snatched the box from him angrily.

"Only three boxes gone?" she repeated. "What have you been doing all day?"

She added to this question a coarse epithet which I shall not repeat.

"I tried to sell them -- indeed I did, Mother Watson, indeed I did -- " said the boy earnestly, "but everybody had bought them already."

"You didn't try," said the woman addressed as Mother Watson. "You're too lazy, that's what's the matter. You didn't earn your salt. Now give me the money."

Mark drew from his pocket a few pennies and handed them to her.

She counted them over, and then looking up sharply said with a frown, "There's a penny short. Where is it?"

"I was so hungry," pleaded Mark, "that I bought an apple -- only a little one."

"You bought an apple, did you?" said the woman menacingly. "So that's the way you spend my money, you little thief?"

"I was so faint and hungry," again pleaded the boy.

"What business had you to be hungry? Didn't you have some breakfast this morning?"

"I had a piece of bread."

"That's more than you earned. You'll eat me out of house and home, you little thief! But I'll pay you off. I'll give you something to take away your appetite. You won't be hungry any more, I reckon."

She drove her flabby hand into her pocket and produced a strap, at which the boy gazed with a frightened look.

"Don't beat me, Mother Watson," he said imploringly.

"I'll beat the laziness out of you," said the woman vindictively. "See if I don't."

She clutched Mark by the collar and was about to bring the strap down forcibly on his back, ill protected by his thin jacket, when a visitor entered the room.

"What's the matter, Mrs. Watson?" asked the intruder.

"Oh, it's you, Mrs. Flanagan?" said the woman holding the strap suspended in the air. "I'll tell you what's the matter. This little thief has come home, after selling only three boxes of matches the whole day, and I find he's stole a penny to buy an apple with. It's for that I'm goin' to beat him."

Oh, let him alone, the poor lad," said Mrs. Flanagan, who was a warm-hearted Irish woman. "Maybe he was hungry."

"Then why didn't he work? That work can eat."

"Maybe people didn't want to buy."

24

"Well, I can't afford to keep him in his idleness," said Mrs. Watson. "He may go to bed without his supper."

"If he can't sell his matches, maybe people would give him something."

Mrs. Watson evidently thought favorably of this suggestion for, turning to Mark, she said, "Go out again, you little thief, and mind you don't come back in again till you've got twenty-five cents to bring to me. Do you mind that?"

Mark listened but stood irresolute.

"I don't like to beg," he said.

"Don't like to beg!" screamed Mrs. Watson. "Do you mind that, now, Mrs. Flanagan? He's too proud to beg."

"Mother told me never to beg if I could help it," said Mark.

"Well, you can't help it," said the woman flourishing the strap in a threatening manner. "Do you see this?"

"Yes."

"Well, you'll feel it too, if you don't do as I tell you. Go out now."

"I'm so hungry," said Mark. "Won't you give me a piece of bread?"

"Not a mouthful till you bring back twenty-five cents. Start now, or you'll feel the strap."

The boy left the room with a slow step and wearily descended the stairs. I hope my young readers will never know the hungry craving for food which tormented the poor boy as he made his way towards the street. But he had hardly reached the foot of the first staircase when he heard a low voice behind him and, turning, beheld Mrs. Flanagan, who had hastily followed after him.

"Are you very hungry?" she asked.

"Yes, I'm faint with hunger."

"Poor boy!" she said compassionately. "Come in here a minute."

She opened the door of her own room which was just at the foot of the staircase and gently pushed him in.

It was a room of the same general appearance as the one above but was much neater looking.

"Biddy Flanagan isn't the woman to let a poor motherless child go hungry when she's a bit of bread or meat by her. Here, Mark, lad. Sit down, and I'll bring you something that'll warm your poor little stomach."

25

She opened a cupboard and brought out a plate containing a small quantity of cold beef and two slices of bread.

"There's some better meat than you'll get off Mother Watson. It's cold, but it's good."

"She never gives any meat at all," said Mark, gazing with a look of eager anticipation at the plate which to his famished eye looked so inviting.

"I'll be bound she don't," said Mrs. Flanagan. "Talk of you being lazy! What does she do herself but sit all day doing nothin' except drink whisky from the black bottle! She might get washin' to do, as I do, if she wanted to, but she won't work. She expects you to get money enough for both of you."

Meanwhile Mrs. Flanagan had poured out a cup of tea from an old tin teapot that stood on the stove.

"There, drink that, Mark dear," she said. "It'll warm you up, and you'll need it this cold night, I'm thinking."

The tea was not of the best quality, and the cup was cracked and discolored, but to Mark it was grateful and refreshing, and he eagerly drank it.

"Is it good?" asked the sympathizing woman, observing with satisfaction the eagerness with which it was drunk.

"Yes, it makes me feel warm," said Mark.

"It's better than the whisky Mother Watson drinks," said Mrs. Flanagan. "It won't make your nose red like hers. It would be a sight better for her if she'd throw away the whisky and take to the tea."

"You are very kind, Mrs. Flanagan," said Mark rising from the table, feeling fifty percent better than when he sat down.

"Oh, bother now, don't say a word about it! Sure you're welcome to the bit you've eaten and the cup of tea. Come in again when you feel hungry, and Bridget Flanagan won't be the woman to send you off hungry if she's got anything in the cupboard."

"I wish Mother Watson was as good as you are," said Mark.

"I ain't so good as I might be," said Mrs. Flanagan, "but I wouldn't be guilty of treatin' a poor boy as that woman treats you, more shame to her! How came you with her any way? She ain't your mother, is she?"

"No," said Mark shuddering at the bare idea. "My mother was a good woman and worked hard. She didn't drink whisky. Mother was always kind to me. I wish she was alive now."

"When did she die, Mark dear?"

"It's going on a year since she died. I didn't know what to do, but Mother Watson told me to come and live with her and she'd take care of me."

"Sorry bit of kindness there was in that," commented Mrs. Flanagan. "She wanted you to take care of her. Well, and what did she make you do?"

"She sent me out to earn what I could. Sometimes I would run on errands, but lately I have sold matches."

"Is it hard work sellin' them?"

"Some days I do pretty well, but some days it seems as if nobody wants any. Today I went round to a great many offices, but they had as many as they wanted, and I didn't sell but three boxes. I tried to sell more, indeed I did, but I couldn't."

"No doubt you did, Mark dear. How cold you must be, in that thin jacket of yours in this cold weather. I've got a shawl you may wear if you like. You'll not lose it, I know."

But Mark had a natural dislike of being dressed as a girl, knowing, moreover, that his appearance in the street with Mrs. Flanagan's shawl would subject him to the jeers of the street boys. So he declined the offer with thanks and, buttoning up his thin jacket, descended the remaining staircase and went out again into the chilling and uninviting street. A chilling, drizzling rain had just set in, and this made it even more dreary than it had been during the day.

CHAPTER VI

BEN GIBSON

But it was not so much the storm or the cold weather that Mark did not care for. He had become used to these, so far as one can be used to what is very disagreeable. If after a hard day's work, he had had a good home to come back to or a kind and sympathizing friend, he would have had that thought to cheer him up. But Mother Watson cared nothing for him except for the money he brought her, and Mark found it impossible either to cherish love or respect for the coarse woman whom he generally found more or less effected by whisky.

Cold and hungry as he had been oftentimes, he had always shrunk from begging. It seemed to lower him in his own thoughts to ask charity of others. Mother Watson had suggested it to him once or twice but had never actually commanded it before. Now he was required to bring home twenty-five cents. He knew very well what would be the result if he failed to do this. Mother Watson would apply the leather strap with merciless fury, and he knew that his strength was nothing compared to hers. So, for the first time in his life, he felt that he must make up his mind to beg.

He retraced his steps to the head of Frankfort Street and walked slowly down Nassau Street. The rain was falling, as I have said, and those who could remained under shelter. Besides, business hours were over. The thousands, who during the day made the lower part of the city busy, had gone to their homes in the upper portion of the island or across the river to Brooklyn or the towns on the Jersey shore. So, however willing he might be to beg, there did not seem to be much chance at present.

The rain increased, and Mark in his thin clothes was soon drenched to the skin. He felt damp, cold and uncomfortable. But there was no rest for him. The only home he had was shut to him unless he should bring home twenty-five cents, and of this there seemed little prospect.

At the corner of Fulton Street he fell in with a boy of twelve, short and sturdy in frame, and dressed in a coat whose tails nearly reached the sidewalk. Though scarcely in the fashion, it was warmer than Mark's, and the proprietor troubled himself very little about the looks.

This boy, whom Mark recognized as Ben Gibson, had a clay pipe in his mouth which he seemed to be smoking with evident enjoyment.

"Where you goin'?" he asked halting in front of Mark.

"I don't know," said Mark.

"Don't know!" repeated Ben, taking his pipe from his mouth and spitting. "Where's your matches?"

"I left them at home."

"Then what'd you come out for in this storm?"

"The woman I live with won't let me come home till I've brought her twenty-five cents."

How'd you expect to get it?"

"She wants me to beg."

"That's the way," said Ben approvingly. "When you get hold of a soft chap or a lady, them's the ones to shell out."

"I don't like it," said Mark. "I don't want people to think me a beggar."

"What's the odds?" said Ben philosophically. "You're just the chap to make a good beggar."

"What do you mean by that, Ben?" said Mark, who was far from considering this much a compliment.

"Why you're a thin, pale little chap that people will pity easy. Now I ain't the right cut for a beggar. I tried it once, but it was no go."

"Why not?" asked Mark, who began to be interested in spite of himself.

"You see," said Ben, again puffing out a volume of smoke, "I look too tough, as if I could take care of myself. People don't pity me. I tried it one night when I was hard up. I hadn't got but six cents, and I wanted to go to the Old Bowery bad. So I went up to a gent as he was comin' up Wall Street from the ferry and said, 'Won't you give a poor boy a few pennies to save him from starvin'?'"

"'So you're almost starvin', are you my lad?' says he.

"'Yes, sir,' said I as faint as I could.

"'Well, starvin' seems to agree with you,' says he laughin'. 'You're the healthiest-looking beggar I've seen in a good while.'

"I tried it again on another gent, and he told me he guessed I was lazy, that a good stout boy like me ought to work. So I didn't make much beggin' and had to give up goin' to the Bowery that night which I was precious sorry for, for there was a great benefit that evenin'. Been there often?"

"No, I never went."

"Never went to the Old Bowery!" cried Ben, whistling in amazement. "Where were you raised, I'd like to know? I should think you was a country greeny, I should."

"I never had the chance," said Mark, who began to feel a little ashamed of the confession.

"Won't your old woman let you go?"

"I never had any money to go."

The Old Bowery Theatre opened in 1826 and showed plays until it burnt down in 1929.

"If I was flush I'd take you myself. It's only fifteen cents," said Ben. "But I haven't got money enough except for one ticket. I'm goin' tonight."

"Are you?" asked Mark a little enviously.

"Yes, it's a good way to pass a rainy evenin'. You've got a warm room to be in, let alone the play which is splendid. Now, if you could only beg fifteen cents from some charitable cove, you might go along with me."

"If I get any money I've got to carry it home."

"Suppose you don't. Will the old woman cut up rough?"

"She'll beat me with a strap," said Mark shuddering.

"What makes you let her do it?" demanded Ben rather disdainfully.

"I can't help it."

"She wouldn't beat me," said Ben decidedly.

"What would you do?" asked Mark with interest.

"What would I do?" retorted Ben. "I'd kick and bite and give her one for herself between the eyes. That's what I'd do. She'd find me a hard case, I reckon."

"It wouldn't be any use for me to try that," said Mark. "She's too strong."

"It don't take much to handle you," said Ben, taking a critical survey of the physical points of Mark. "You're most light enough to blow away."

"I'm only ten years old," said Mark apologetically. "I shall be bigger some time."

"Maybe," said Ben dubiously, "but you don't look as if you'd ever be tough like me."

"There," he added after a pause. "I've smoked all my 'baccy. I wish I'd got some more."

"Do you like to smoke?" asked Mark.

"It warms a feller up," said Ben. "It's jest the thing for a cold, wet day like this. Didn't you ever try it?"

"No."

"If I'd got some 'baccy here, I'd give you a whiff, but I think it would make you sick the first time."

"I don't think I should like it," said Mark, who had never felt any desire to smoke though he knew plenty of boys who indulged in the habit.

"That's because you don't know nothin' about it," remarked Ben. "I didn't like it at first till I got learned."

"Do you smoke often?"

"Every day after I get through blackin' boots -- that is, when I ain't hard up and can raise the stamps to pay for the 'baccy. But I guess I'll be goin' up to the Old Bowery. It's almost time for the doors to open. Where you goin'?"

"I don't know where to go,' said Mark helplessly.

"I'll tell you where you'd better go. You won't find nobody round here. Besides it ain't comfortable lettin' the rain fall on you and wet you through." (While this conversation was going on, the boys had sheltered themselves in a doorway.) "Just you go down to Fulton Market. There you'll be out of the wet, and you'll see plenty of people passin' through when the boats come in. Maybe some of 'em will give you somethin'. Then ag'in, there's the boats. Some nights I sleep aboard the boats."

"You do? Will they let you?"

"They don't notice. I just pay my two cents and go aboard and snuggle up in a corner and go to sleep. So I ride to Brooklyn and back all night. That's cheaper'n the Newsboy's Lodgin' House for it only costs two cents. One night a gentleman came to me and woke me up and said, 'We've got to Brooklyn, my lad. If you don't get up they'll carry you back again.'

"I jumped up and told him I was much obliged as I didn't know what my family would say if I didn't get home by eleven o'clock. Then, just as soon as his back was turned, I sat down again and went to sleep. It ain't so bad sleepin' aboard the boat, 'specially on a cold night. They keep the cabin warm, and though the seat isn't partic'larly soft, it's better'n bein' out in the street. If you don't get your twenty-five cents and are afraid of a lickin', you'd better sleep aboard the boat."

"Perhaps I will," said Mark, to whom the idea was not unwelcome for it would at all events save him for that night from the beating which would be his portion if he came home without the required sum.

"Well, good night," said Ben. "I'll be goin' along."

"Good night, Ben," said Mark. "I guess I'll go to Fulton Market."

Accordingly Mark turned down Fulton Street while Ben steered in the direction of Clatham Street, through which it was necessary to pass in order to reach the theater which is situated on the Bowery not far from its junction with Clatham Street.

Ben Gibson is a type of a numerous class of improvident boys who live on from day to day careless of appearances, spending their evenings where they can -- at the theater when their means admit and sometimes at gambling saloons. Not naturally bad, they drift into bad habits from the force of outward circumstances. They learn early to smoke or chew, finding in tobacco some comfort during the cold and wet days, either ignorant of or indifferent to the harm which the insidious weed will do to their constitution. So, their growth is checked or their blood is impoverished as is shown by their pale faces.

As for Ben, he was gifted with a sturdy frame and an excellent constitution and appeared as yet to exhibit none of the baneful effects of this habit. But no growing boy can smoke without ultimately being affected by it and such will no doubt be the case with Ben.

CHAPTER VII

FULTON MARKET

Just across from Fulton Ferry stands Fulton Market. It is nearly fifty years old, having been built in 1821 on ground formerly occupied by unsightly wooden buildings which were, perhaps fortunately, swept away by fire. It covers the block bounded by Fulton, South, Beekman, and Front Streets and was erected at the cost of about a quarter of a million dollars.

This is the chief of the great city markets, and an immense business is done here. There is hardly an hour in the twenty-four in which there is an entire lull in the business of the place. Some of the outside shops and booths are kept open all night, while the supplies of fish, meats, and vegetables for the market proper are brought at a very early hour, almost before it can be called morning.

Besides the market proper the surrounding sidewalks are roofed over and lined with shops and booths of the most diverse character at which almost every conceivable article can be purchased. Most numerous, perhaps, are the chief restaurants where the counters are loaded with cakes and pies and a steaming vessel of coffee smoking at one end. The floors are sanded, and the accommodations are far from elegant or luxurious, but it is said that the food is by no means to be despised. Then there are fruit stalls with tempting heaps of oranges, apples, and, in their season, the fruits of summer, presided over for the most part by old women who shrewdly scan the faces of passers-by and are ready on the smallest provocation to vaunt the merits of their wares. There are candy and coconut cakes for those who have a sweet tooth, and many a shop boy invests in these on his way to or from Brooklyn to the New York store where he is employed; or the father of a family, on his way to his Brooklyn home, thinks of the little ones awaiting him and indulges in a purchase of what he knows will sure to be acceptable to them.

Fulton Market in the late 1800s or early 1900s.

But it is not only the wants of the body that are provided for at Fulton Market. On the Fulton Street side may be found extensive booths at which are displayed for sale a tempting array of papers, magazines, and books, as well as stationery, photograph albums, etc., generally at prices twenty or thirty percent lower than is demanded for them in the more pretentious Broadway or Fulton Avenue stores.

Even at night, therefore, the outer portion of the market, securely roofed over and well lighted, presents a bright and cheerful shelter from the inclement weather, while some of the booths are kept open however late the hour.

Ben Gibson, therefore, was right in directing Mark to Fulton Market as probably the most comfortable place to be found in the pouring rain which made the thoroughfares dismal and dreary. Mark, of course, had been in Fulton Market often and saw at once the wisdom of the advice. He ran down Fulton Street as fast as he could and arrived there panting and wet to the skin. Uncomfortable as he was, the change from the wet streets to the bright and comparatively warm shelter of the market made him at once more cheerful. In fact, it compared favorably with the cold and uninviting room which he shared with Mother Watson.

As Mark looked around him, he could not help wishing that he tended in one of the little restaurants that looked so bright and inviting to him. Those who are accustomed to lunch at Delmonico's or at some of the large and stylish hotels, or those who have their meals served by attentive servants in brown stone dwellings in the more fashionable quarters of the city, would be likely to turn up their noses at his humble taste and would feel it an infliction to take a meal amid such plebeian surroundings. But then Mark knew nothing about the fare at Delmonico's and was far enough from living in a brown stone front, and so his ideas of happiness and luxury were not very exalted, or he would scarcely have envied the stout butcher boy whom he saw sitting at an unpainted wooden table partaking in a repast which was more abundant than choice.

But from the surrounding comfort Mark's thoughts were brought back to a disagreeable business which brought him here. He was to solicit charity from some one of the passers-by, and with a sigh he began to look about him to select some compassionate face.

"If there was only somebody here that wanted an errand done," he thought, "and would pay me twenty-five cents for doing it, I wouldn't have to beg. I'd rather work two hours for the money than beg for it."

But there seemed little chance of this. In the busy portion of the day there might have been some chance -- though this would be uncertain -- but now it was very improbable. If he wanted to get twenty-five cents that night, he must get it from charity.

A beginning must be made, however disagreeable. So Mark went up to a young man who was passing along on his way to the boat, and in a shamefaced manner he said, "Will you give me some pennies, please?"

The young man looked good-natured, and it was that which gave Mark confidence to address him.

"You want pennies, do you?" he said with a smile, pausing in his walk.

"If you please, sir."

"I suppose your wife and family are starving, eh?"

"I haven't got and wife or family, sir," said Mark.

"But you've got a sick mother or some brothers or sisters that are starving, haven't you?"

"No, sir."

"Then I'm afraid you're not up to your business. How long have you been round begging?"

"Never before," said Mark rather indignantly.

"Ah, that accounts for it. You haven't learned the business yet. After a few weeks you'll have a sick mother starving at home. They all do, you know."

"My mother is dead," said Mark. "I shan't tell a lie to get money."

"Come, you're a rather remarkable boy," said the young man, a reporter on a daily paper going over to attend a meeting in Brooklyn to write an account of it to appear in one of the city dailies in the morning. "I don't generally give money in such cases, but I must make an exception in your case."

He drew a dime from his vest pocket and handed it to Mark.

Mark took it with a blush of mortification at the necessity.

"I wouldn't beg if I could help it," he said, desiring to justify himself in the eyes of the good-natured young man.

"I'm glad to hear that, Johnny." (Johnny is a common name applied to boys whose names are unknown.) "It isn't a very creditable business. What makes you beg, then?"

"I shall be beaten if I don't," said Mark.

"That's bad. Who will beat you?"

"Mother Watson."

"Tell Mother Watson, with my compliments, that she's a wicked old tyrant. I'll tell you what, my lad, you must grow as fast as you can, and by and by you'll get too large for that motherly old woman to whip. But there goes the bell. I must be getting aboard."

This was the result of Mark's first begging appeal. He looked at the money and wished he had got it in any other way. If it had been the reward of an hour's work, he would have gazed at it with much greater satisfaction.

Well, he had made a beginning. He had got ten cents. But there still remained fifteen cents to obtain, and without that he did not feel safe in going back.

So he looked about him for another person to address. This time he thought he would ask a lady. Accordingly he went up to one, who was walking with her son, a boy of sixteen to judge from appearance, and asked for a few pennies.

"Get out of my way, you little beggar!" she said in a disagreeable tone. "Ain't you ashamed of yourself, going round begging, instead of earning money like honest people?"

"I've been trying to earn money all day," said Mark, rather indignant at this attack.

"Oh, no doubt," sneered the woman. "I don't think you'll hurt yourself with work."

"I was round the streets all day trying to sell matches," said Mark.

"You mustn't believe what he says, mother," said the boy. "They're all a set of humbugs and will lie as fast as they can talk."

"I've no doubt of it, Roswell," said Mrs. Crawford. "Such little impostors never get anything out of me. I've got other uses for my money."

Mark was a gentle, peaceful boy, but such attacks naturally made him indignant.

"I am not an impostor, and I neither lie nor steal," he said, looking alternately from the mother to the son.

"Oh, you're a fine young man, I've no doubt," said Roswell with a sneer. "But we'd better be getting on, mother, unless you mean to stop in Fulton Market all night."

So mother and son passed on, leaving Mark with a sense of mortification and injury. He would have given the ten cents he had not to have asked charity of this woman who had answered him so unpleasantly.

Those of my readers who have read the two preceding volumes of this series will recognize in Roswell Crawford and his mother old acquaintances who played an important part of the former stories. As, however, I may have some new readers, it may be as well to explain that Roswell was a self-conceited boy, who prided himself on being "the son of a gentleman," and whose great desire was to find a job where the pay would be large and the duties very small. Unfortunately for his pride, his father had failed in business shortly before he died, and his mother had been compelled to keep a boarding house. She, too, was troubled with a pride very similar to that of her son and chafed inwardly at her position instead of reconciling herself to it as many better persons have done.

Roswell was not very fortunate in retaining the jobs he obtained, being generally averse to doing anything except what he was absolutely obliged to do. He had lost a job in a dry goods store on Sixth Avenue because he objected to carrying bundles, considering it beneath the dignity of a gentleman's son. Some months before he had tried to get Richard Hunter discharged from his job in the hope of succeeding him in it, but this plot proved utterly unsuccessful as is fully described in "Fame and Fortune."

We shall have more to do with Roswell Crawford in the course of the present story. At present he was employed in a retail bookstore uptown on a salary of six dollars a week.

CHAPTER VIII

ON THE FERRYBOAT

Mark had made two applications for charity and still had but ten cents. The manner in which Mrs. Crawford met his appeal made the business seem more disagreeable than ever. Besides, he was getting tired. It was not more than eight o'clock, but he had been up early and had been on his feet all day. He leaned against one of the stalls, but in so doing he aroused the suspicions of the vigilant old woman who presided over it.

"Just stand away there," she said. "You're watchin' for a chance to steal one of them apples."

"No, I'm not," said Mark indignantly. "I never steal."

"Don't tell me," said the old woman, who had a hearty aversion to boys, some of whom, it must be confessed, had at times played mean tricks on her. "Don't tell me! Them that beg will steal, and I see you beggin' just now."

To this Mark had no reply to make. He saw that he was already classed with the young street beggars, many of whom, as the old woman implied, had no particular objection to stealing if they got a chance. Altogether he was so disgusted with his new business that he felt it impossible for him to beg anymore that night. But then came up the consideration that this would prevent his returning home. He very well knew what kind of a reception Mother Watson would give him, and he had a very unpleasant recollection and terror of the leather strap.

But where should he go? He must pass the night somewhere, and he already felt drowsy. Why should he not follow Ben Gibson's suggestions and sleep on the Fulton ferryboat? It would only cost two cents to get on board, and he might ride all night. Fortunately he had more than money enough for that, though he did not like to think how he came by the ten cents.

When Mark had made up his mind, he passed out of one of the entrances of the market and, crossing the street, presented his ten cents at the wicket where stood the fare-taker.

Without a look towards him, the functionary took the money and pushed back eight cents. These Mark took and passed round into the large room of the ferry house.

The boat was not in, but he already saw it halfway across the river speeding towards its pier.

Before the Brooklyn Bridge was completed in 1883, ferryboats were used to cross between Manhattan and Brooklyn on the East River.

There were few persons waiting besides himself, for the great rush of travel was diminished for a short time. It would set in again about eleven o'clock when those who had passed the evening at some place of amusement in New York would be on their way home.

Mark, with the rest, waited till the boat reached its wharf. There was the usual bump, and then the chain rattled, the wheel went round, and the passengers began to pour out onto the wharf. Mark passed into the boat and went at once to the "gentleman's cabin" situated on the left-hand side of the boat. Generally, however, gentlemen rather unfairly crowd into the ladies' cabin, sometimes compelling the ladies, to whom it rightfully belongs, to stand, while they complacently monopolize the seats. The gentleman's cabin, so called, is occupied by those who have a little more regard to the rights of ladies and by the smokers who are at liberty to indulge in their favorite comfort here.

When Mark entered the air was heavy with tobacco smoke, generally emitted from clay pipes and cheap cigars and therefore not so agreeable as it might have been under other circumstances. But it was warm and comfortable, and that was a good deal.

In the corner Mark espied a whole seat nearly double the size of an ordinary seat, and this he decided would make the most comfortable niche for him.

He settled himself down there as well as he could. The seat was hard and not so comfortable as it might have been, but then Mark was not accustomed to beds of down, and he was so weary that his eyes closed and he was soon in the land of dreams.

He was dimly conscious of the arrival at the Brooklyn side and the ensuing hurried exit of passengers from that part of the cabin in which he was; but it was only a slight interruption, and when the boat, having set out on its homeward trip, reached the New York side he was fast asleep.

"Poor little fellow!" thought more than one with a hasty glance at the sleeping boy. "He is taking his comfort where he can."

But there was no good Samaritan to take him by the hand and inquire into his hardships and provide for his necessities; or rather there was one, and that one well known to us.

Richard Hunter and his friend Henry Fosdick had been to Brooklyn that evening to attend an instructive lecture which they had seen announced in one of the daily papers. The lecture concluded at half-past nine, and they took the ten o'clock boat over the Fulton Ferry.

They seated themselves in the first cabin towards the Brooklyn side and did not, therefore, see Mark until they passed through the other cabin on the arrival of the boat at New York.

"Look there, Fosdick," said Richard Hunter. "See that poor little chap asleep in the corner. Doesn't it remind you of the times we used to have when we were as badly off as he?"

"Yes, Dick, but I don't think I ever slept on a ferryboat."

"That's because you were not on the streets long. I took care of myself eight years and more than once took a cheap bed for two cents on a boat like this. Most likely I've slept in that very corner."

"It was a hard life, Dick."

"Yes, and a hard bed, too. But there's a good many that are no better off now. I always feel like doing something to help along those like this little chap here."

"I wonder what he is. A bootblack?"

"He hasn't any brush or box with him. Perhaps he's a newsboy. I think I'll give him a surprise."

"Wake him up, do you mean?"

"No, poor little chap! Let him sleep. I'll put fifty cents in his pocket, and when he wakes up he won't know where it came from."

"That's a good idea, Dick. I'll do the same. All right. Here's the money. Put mine in with yours. Don't wake him up."

Dick walked softly up to the match boy, and gently inserted the money -- one dollar -- in one of the pockets of his ragged vest.

42

Mark was so fast asleep that he was entirely unconscious of the benevolent act.

"That'll make him open his eyes in the morning," he said.

"Unless somebody relieves him of the money during his sleep."

"Not much chance of that. Pickpockets won't be very apt to meddle with such a ragged chap as that, unless its in a fit of temporary aberration of mind."

"You're right, Dick. But we must hurry out now, or we shall be carried back to Brooklyn."

"And so get more than our money's worth. I wouldn't want to cheat the corporation so extensively as that."

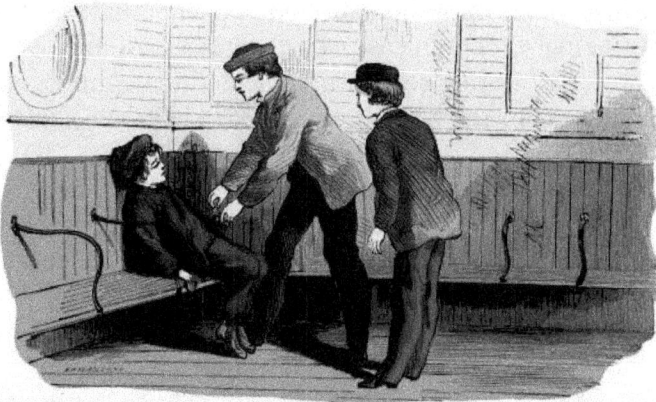

Dick as a philanthropist.

So the two friends passed out of the boat and left the match boy asleep in the cabin, quite unconscious that good fortune had hovered over him, and made him richer by a dollar, while he slept.

While we are waiting for him to awake, we may as well follow Richard Hunter and his friend home.

Fosdick's good fortune, which we recorded in the earlier chapters of this volume, had made no particular change in their arrangements. They were already living in better style than was usual among youths situated as they were. There was this difference, however, that whereas formerly Dick paid the greater part of the joint expense it was now divided equally. It will be remembered that Fosdick's interest on the twenty bank shares purchased in his name amounted to one hundred and sixty dollars annually, and this just about enabled him to pay his own way, though not leaving him a large surplus for clothing and incidental expenses. It could not be long, however, before his pay would be increased at the store, probably by two dollars a week. Until that time he could economize a little for upon one thing he had made up his mind: not to trench upon his principal except in case of sickness or absolute necessity.

The boys had not forgotten or neglected the commission which they had undertaken for Mr. Hiram Bates. They had visited, on the evening after he left, the Newsboys' Lodging House -- then located at the corner of Fulton and Nassau Streets in the upper part of the Sun building -- and had consulted Mr. O'Connor, the efficient superintendent, as to the boy of whom they were in search. But he had no information to supply them with. He promised to inquire among the boys who frequented the lodge, as it was possible that there might be some among them who might have fallen in with a boy named Talbot.

Richard Hunter also sought out some of his old acquaintances, who were still engaged in blacking boots or selling newspapers, and offered a reward of five dollars for the discovery of a boy of ten named Talbot or John Talbot.

As the result of this offer a red-haired boy was brought round to the counting room one day who stoutly asserted that his name was John Talbot, and his guide in consequence claimed the reward. Dick, however, had considerable doubt as to the genuineness of his claim and called the errand boy, known to the readers of earlier volumes as Mickey Maguire.

"Micky," said Richard, "this boy says he is John Talbot. Do you know him?"

"Know him!" repeated Micky. "I've knowed him ever since he was so high. He's no more John Talbot than I am. His name is Tim Hogan, and I'll defy him to say it isn't."

44

Tim looked guilty, and his companion gave up the attempt to obtain the promised reward. He had hired Tim by the promise of a dollar to say he was John Talbot, hoping by the means to clear four dollars for himself.

"That boy'll rise to a seat in the Common Council if he lives long enough," said Dick. "He's an unusually promising specimen."

CHAPTER IX

A PLEASANT DISCOVERY

The night wore away, and still Mark, the match boy, continued to sleep soundly in the corner of the cabin where he had established himself. One of the boat hands passing through noticed him and was on the point of waking him but, observing his weary look and thin attire, refrained from an impulse of compassion. He had a boy of about the same age, and the thought came to him that some time his boy might be placed in the same situation, and this warmed his heart towards the little vagrant.

"I suppose I ought to wake him up," he reflected. "but he isn't doing any harm there, and he may as well have his sleep out."

So Mark slept on -- a merciful sleep, in which he forgot his poverty and friendless condition, a sleep which brought new strength and refreshment to his limbs.

When he woke up it was six o'clock in the morning. But it was quite dark still for it was in December, and, so far as appearances went, it might have been midnight. But already sleepy men and boys were on their way to the great city to their daily work. Some were employed a considerable distance uptown and must be at their posts at seven. Others were employed in the markets and must be stirring at an early hour. There were keepers of street stands who liked to be ready for the first wave in the tide of daily travel that was to sweep through the city streets without interruption until late at night. So altogether, even at this early hour, there was quite a number of passengers.

Mark rubbed his eyes, not quite sure where he was or how he got there. He half expected to hear the harsh voice of Mother Watson, which usually aroused him to his daily toil. But there was no Mother Watson to be seen -- only sleepy, gaping men and boys, clad in working dress.

Mark sat up and looked around him.

"Well, young chap, you've had a nap, haven't you?" said a man at his side, who appeared, from a strong smell of paint about his clothes, to be a journeyman painter.

"Yes," said Mark. "Is it morning?"

"To be sure it is. What did you expect it was?"

46

"Then I've been sleeping all night," said the match boy in surprise.

"Where?"

"Here."

"In that corner?" asked the painter.

"Yes," said Mark. "I came aboard last night and fell asleep, and that's the last I remember."

"It must be rather hard to the bones," said the painter. "I think that I should prefer a regular bed."

"I do feel sore," said the match boy, "but I slept bully."

"A little chap like you can curl up anywhere. I don't think I could sleep very well on those seats. Haven't you got any home?"

"Yes," said Mark, "a sort of a home."

"Then why didn't you sleep at home?"

"I knew I should get a beating if I went home without twenty-five cents."

"Well, that's hard luck. I wonder how I should feel," he continued, laughing, "if my wife gave me a beating when I came home short of funds."

But here the usual bump indicated the arrival of the boat at the slip, and all the passengers, the painter included, rose and hurried to the edge of the boat.

With the rest went Mark. He had no particular object in going this early, but his sleep was over and there was no inducement to remain longer in the boat.

The rain was over also. The streets were still wet from the effects of the quantity that had fallen, but there was no prospect of any more. Mark's wet clothes had dried in the warm, dry atmosphere of the cabin, and he felt considerably better than on the evening previous.

Now, however, he could not help wondering what Mother Watson had thought of his absence.

"She'll be mad, I know," he thought. "I suppose she'll whip me when I get back."

This certainly was not a pleasant thought. The leather strap was an old enemy of his which he dreaded, and with good reason. He was afraid that he would get a more severe beating, for not having returned the night before, at the hands of the angry old woman.

"I wish I didn't live with Mother Watson," he thought.

Straight upon this thought came another. "Why should I?"

Mother Watson had no claim on him. Upon his mother's death she had assumed the charge of him but, as it turned out, rather for her own advantage than his. She had taken all his earnings and given him in return a share of her miserable apartment and a crust of bread or two, daily seasoned with occasional assaults from the leather strap. It had never occurred to Mark before, but now, for the first time, it dawned upon him that he had the worst of the bargain. He could live more comfortable by retaining his earnings and spending them upon himself.

Mark was rather a timid, mild-mannered boy, or he would sooner have rebelled against the tyranny and abuse of Mother Watson. But he had had little confidence in himself and wanted somebody to lean on. In selecting the old woman, who had acted thus far as his guardian, he had leaned upon a broken reed. The last night's experience gave him a little courage. He reflected that he could sleep in the Newsboys' Lodging House for five cents or on the ferryboat again for two, while the fare at his old home was hardly so sumptuous, and he could obtain the same without very large expense.

So Mark thought seriously of breaking his yoke and declaring himself free and independent, a discovery which he confirmed in his half-formed resolution.

He remembered that after paying his toll he had eight cents left, which he had placed in his vest pocket. He thought that those would enable him to get some breakfast and drew them out. To his astonishment there were two silver half-dollars mingled with the coppers. Mark opened his eyes wide in astonishment. Where could they have come from? Was it possible that the tollman had given him them by mistake for pennies? That could not be, for two reasons: first, he remembered looking at the change as it was handed him, and he knew that there were no half-dollars among them; second, the eight pennies were all there, the silver coins making the number ten.

It was certainly very strange and surprising and puzzled Mark not a little. We, who know all about it, find the explanation very easy, but to the little match boy it was an unfathomable mystery.

The surprise, however, was of an agreeable character. With so much money in his possession, Mark felt like a man with a handsome balance at his banker's, and with the usual elasticity of youth he did not look forward to the time when this supply would be exhausted.

"I won't go back to Mother Watson," he determined. "She's beaten me times enough. I'll take care of myself."

While these thoughts were passing through his mind, he had walked up Fulton Street and reached the corner of Nassau. Here he met his friend of the night before, Ben Gibson.

Ben looked rather sleepy. He had been at the Old Bowery Theater the night before until twelve o'clock and had crept into a corner of the Times printing office and slept but had not quite slept off his fatigue.

"Hallo, young 'un!" said he. "Where did you come from?"

"From Fulton Ferry," said Mark. "I slept on the boat."

"Did you? How'd you like it?"

"Pretty good," said Mark. "It was rather hard."

"How'd you make out begging?"

"Not very well. I got ten cents."

"So you didn't dare go home to the old woman?"

"I shan't go home there anymore," said the match boy.

"Do you mean it?"

"Yes, I do."

"Bully for you! I like your pluck. I wouldn't go back and get a licking, if I were you. What'll Mother Watson say?"

"She'll be mad, I expect," said Mark.

"Keep a sharp lookout for her. I'll tell you what you can do: stay near me, and if she comes prowlin' round I'll manage her."

"Could you?" said Mark quickly, who, from certain recollections, had considerable fear of his stout tyrant.

"You may just bet on that. What you goin' to do?"

"I think I shall go and get some breakfast," said Mark.

"So would I, if I had any tin, but I'm dead broke -- spent my last cent goin' to the Old Bowery. I'll have to wait till I've had one or two shines before I can eat breakfast."

"Are you hungry?"

"I'll bet I am."

"Because," said Mark hesitating, "I'll lend you money enough for breakfast, and you can pay me when you earn it."

"You lend me money!" exclaimed Ben in astonishment. "Why, you haven't got but eight cents."

"Yes, I have," said Mark producing the two half-dollars.

"Where's you get them?" asked the bootblack in unfeigned surprise, looking at Mark as if he had all at once developed into an Astor or Stewart.

"You haven't been begging this morning, have you?"

"No," said the match boy, "and I don't mean to beg again if I can help it."

"Then where'd you get the money?"

"I don't know."

"Don't know! You haven't been stealin', have you?"

Mark disclaimed the imputation indignantly.

"Then you found a pocketbook?"

"No, I didn't."

"Then where did you get the money?"

"I don't know any more than you do. When I went to sleep on the boat I didn't have it, but this morning when I felt in my pocket it was there."

"That's mighty strange," said Ben whistling.

"So I think."

"It's good money, ain't it?"

"Try it and see."

Ben tossed up one of the coins. It fell with a clear, ringing sound on the sidewalk.

"Yes, that's good," he said. "I just wish somebody'd treat me that way. Maybe it's the vest. If 'tis I'd like to buy it."

"I don't think it's that," said Mark laughing.

"Anyway you've got the money. I'll borrow twenty cents from you, and we'll go and get some breakfast."

CHAPTER X

ON THE WAR PATH

Ben led the way to a cheap restaurant where, for eighteen cents, each of the boys got a breakfast which, to their not very fastidious tastes, proved very satisfactory.

"There," said Ben, with a sigh of satisfaction as they rose from the table, "now I feel like work. I'll pay up that money afore night."

"All right," said Mark.

"What are you goin' to do?"

"I don't know," said Mark irresolutely.

"You're a match boy, ain't you?"

"Yes."

"Where's your matches?"

"In Mother Watson's room."

"You might go and get 'em when she's out."

"No," said Mark shaking his head, "I won't do that."

"Why not? You ain't afraid to go round there, be you?"

"It isn't that -- but the matches are hers, not mine."

"What's the odds?"

"I won't take anything of hers."

"Well you can buy some of your own, then. You've got money enough."

"So I will," said Mark. "It's lucky that money came to me in my sleep."

"That's a lucky boat. I guess I'll go there and sleep tonight."

Mark did as he proposed. With the money he had he was able to purchase a good supply of matches, and when it became light enough he began to vend them.

Hitherto he had not been very fortunate in the disposal of his wares, being timid and bashful, but then he was working for Mother Watson and expected to derive very little advantage for himself from his labors. Now he was working for himself, and this seemed to put new spirit and courage into him. Then again he felt that he had shaken off the hateful thralldom in which Mother Watson had held him, and this gave him a hopefulness which he had not before possessed.

The consequence was that at noon he found that he had earned forty cents in addition to his investment. At that time too, Ben was ready to pay him his loan so that Mark found himself twenty-two cents better off than he had been in the morning, having a capital of a dollar and thirty cents, out of which, however, he must purchase his lunch.

While he is getting on in such an encouraging manner we must go back to Mother Watson.

When Mark did not return the night before she grumbled considerably, but no thought of his intentional desertion dawned upon her. Indeed, she had counted upon his timidity and lack of courage, knowing well that a more spirited boy would have broken her chain long before. She only thought, therefore, that he had not got the twenty-five cents and did not dare to come back, especially as she had forbidden him to do so.

So, determining to give him a taste of the leather strap in the morning, she went to bed, first taking a fresh potation from the whisky bottle which was her constant companion.

Late in the morning Mother Watson woke, feeling as usual, at that hour of the day, cross and uncomfortable and with a strong desire to make someone else uncomfortable. But Mark, whom she usually made to bear the burden of her temper, was still away. For the first time the old woman began to feel a little apprehensive that he had deserted her. This was far from suiting her, as she found his earnings very convenient and found it besides pleasant to have somebody to scold.

She hastily dressed, without paying much attention to her hygiene or appearance. Indeed, to do Mother Watson justice, her mind was far from being filled with the vanity of her dress, and if she erred on that subject it was in the opposite extreme.

When her simple wash was accomplished she went downstairs and knocked at Mrs. Flanagan's door.

"Come in!" said a hearty voice.

Mrs. Flanagan was hard at work at her washtub and had been for a good couple of hours. She raised her good-natured face as the old woman entered.

"The top of the morning to you, Mother Watson," she said. "I hope you're in fine health this morning, mum."

"Then you'll be disappointed," said Mrs. Watson. "I've got a bad feeling at my stomach and have it most every morning."

52

"It's the whisky," thought Mrs. Flanagan, but she thought it best not to intimate as much, as it might lead to hostilities.

"Better take a cup of tea," said she.

"I haven't got any," said the old woman. "I wouldn't mind a cup if you've got some handy."

"Sit down then," said Mrs. Flanagan hospitably. "I've got some left from breakfast, only it's cold, but if you'll wait a bit, I'll warm it over for you."

Mother Watson sank into a chair and began to give a full account of her ailments to her neighbor who tried hard to sympathize with her, though, knowing the cause of the ailments, she found this rather difficult.

"Have you seen anything of my boy this morning?" she asked after a while.

"What, Mark?" said Mrs. Flanagan. "Didn't he come home last night?"

"No," said the old woman, "and he isn't home yet. When he does come I'll give him a dose of the strap. He's a bad, lazy, shiftless boy, and worries my life out."

"You're hard on the poor boy, Mother Watson. You must remember he's but a wisp of a lad and hasn't much strength."

"He's strong enough," muttered Mother Watson. "It's lazy he is. Just let him come home, that's all!"

"You told him not to come home unless he had twenty-five cents to bring with him."

"So I did, and why didn't he do it?"

"He couldn't get the money, it's likely, and he's afraid of bein' bate."

"Well, he will be beat then, Mrs. Flanagan, you may be sure of that," said the old woman, diving her hand into her pocket to see that the strap was safe.

"Then you're a bad, cruel woman, to bate that poor motherless child," said Mrs. Flanagan with spirit.

"Say that again, Mrs. Flanagan," exclaimed Mother Watson irefully. "My hearin' isn't as good as it was, and maybe I didn't hear you right."

"No wonder your hearin' isn't good," said Mrs. Flanagan, who now broke bounds completely. "I shouldn't think you'd have any sense left with the whisky you drink."

53

"Perhaps you mean to insult me," said the old woman, glaring at her hostess with one of the frowns which used to send terror to the heart of poor Mark.

"Take it as you please, mum," said Mrs. Flanagan intrepidly. "I'm entirely willin'. I've been wanting to spake mind a long while, and now I've spoke it."

Mother Watson clutched the end of the strap in her pocket and eyed her hostess with a half wish that it would do to treat her as she had treated Mark so often, but Mrs. Flanagan, with her strong arms and sturdy frame, looked like an antagonist not very easily overcome, and Mrs. Watson forbore, though unwillingly.

Meanwhile the tea was beginning to emit quite a savory odor, and the wily old woman thought it best to change her tactics.

Accordingly she burst into tears and, rocking backward and forward, declared that she was a miserable old woman and hadn't a friend in the world, and she succeeded in getting up such a display of misery that the soft heart of Mrs. Flanagan was touched, and she apologized for the unpleasant personal observations she had made and hoped Mother Watson would take tea.

To this Mother Watson finally agreed, and intimating that she was faint, Mrs. Flanagan made some toast for her, of which the cunning old woman partook with exceeding relish, notwithstanding her state of unhappiness.

"Come in any time, Mother Watson," said Mrs. Flanagan, "when you want a sip of tea, I'll be glad to have you take some with me."

"Thank you, Mrs. Flanagan. Maybe I'll look in once in a while. A sip of tea goes to the right spot when I feel bad at my stomach."

"Must you be goin', Mother Watson?"

"Yes," said the old woman. "I'm going out on a little walk, to see my sister that keeps a candy stand by the Park railings. If Mark comes in, will you tell him he'll find the matches upstairs?"

This Mrs. Flanagan promised to do, and the old woman went downstairs and into the street.

But she had not stated her object quite correctly. It was true that she had a sister who was in the confectionery and apple line, presiding over one of the stalls beside the Park railings, but the two sisters were not on very good terms, chiefly because the candy merchant, who was more industrious and correct in her habits than her sister, declined to lend money to Mother Watson -- a refusal which led to a perfect coolness between them. It was not therefore to see her that the old woman went out. She wanted to find Mark. She did not mean to lose her hold upon him, if there was any chance of retaining it, and she therefore made up her mind to visit the places where he was commonly to be found and, when found, to bring him home, by violence if necessary.

So with an old plaid cloak draping from her broad shoulders and her hand grasping the strap in her pocket, she made her way to the square, peering about on all sides with her ferret-like eyes in hope of discovering the missing boy.

CHAPTER XI

MARK'S VICTORY

Meanwhile Mark, rejoicing in his new-found freedom, had started on a business walk among the stores and offices at the lower part of Nassau Street and among the law and banking offices of Wall Street. Fortunately for Mark there had been a rise in stocks, and Wall Street was in good-humor. So a few of the crumbs from the tables of the prosperous bankers and brokers fell in his way. One man, who had just realized ten thousand dollars on a rise in some railway securities, handed Mark fifty cents, but declined to take any of his wares. So this was all clear profit and quite a windfall for the little match boy. Again, in one or two cases he received double price for some of his matches, and the result was that he found himself by eleven o'clock the possessor of two dollars and a quarter, with a few boxes of matches still left.

Mark could hardly realize his own good fortune. Somehow it seemed a great deal more profitable as well as more agreeable to be in business for himself than to be acting as the agent of Mother Watson. Mark determined that he would never go back to her unless he was actually obliged to do so.

He wanted somebody to sympathize with him in his good fortune, and, as he had nearly sold out, he determined to hunt up Ben Gibson and inform him of his run of luck.

Ben, as he knew, was generally to be found on Nassau Street somewhere near the corner of Spruce Street. He therefore turned up Nassau Street from Wall, and in five minutes he reached the business stand of his friend Ben.

Ben had just finished up a job as Mark came up. His patron, it was quite evident, hailed from the country. He wore a blue coat with brass buttons and a tall hat in the style of ten years before with an immense top. He gazed with complacency at the fine polish which Ben had imparted to his boots, a pair of stout cowhides, and inquired with an assumption of indifference, "Well, boy, what's the tax?"

"Twenty-five cents," said Ben coolly.

"Twenty-five cents!" cried the customer with a gasp of amazement. "Come now, you're jokin'."

"No, I ain't," said Ben.

"You don't mean to say you charge twenty-five cents for five-minutes work?"

"Reg'lar price," said Ben.

"Why I don't get but twelve and a half cents an hour when I work out hayin'," said the young man in a tone expressive of his sense of the unfairness to the comparative compensation.

"Maybe you don't have to pay a big license," said Ben.

"A license for blackin' boots?" exclaimed the countryman in surprise.

"Of course. I have to deposit five hundred dollars, more of less, in the city treasury before I can black boots."

"Five--hundred--dollars!" repeated the customer, opening his eyes wide at the information.

"Of course," said Ben. "If I didn't they'd put me in jail for a year."

"And does he pay a license too?" asked the countryman pointing to Mark, who had just come up.

"He only has to pay two hundred and fifty dollars," said Ben. "They ain't so hard on him as on us."

The young man drew out his wallet reluctantly and managed to raise twenty-three cents which he handed to Ben.

"I wouldn't have had my boots blackened, if I'd known the price," he said. "I could have blackened 'em myself at home. They didn't cost but three dollars, and it don't pay to give twenty-five cents to have 'em blackened."

"It'll make 'em last twice as long," said Ben. "My blacking is the superiorest kind and keeps boots from wearin' out."

"I haven't got the other two cents," said the young man. "Ain't that near enough?"

"It'll do," said Ben magnanimously, "seein' you didn't know the price."

The victimized customer walked away gratified to have saved the two cents but hardly reconciled to have expended almost quarter of a dollar on a piece of work which he might have done himself before leaving home.

"Well, what luck, Mark?" said Ben. "I took in that chap neat, didn't I?"

"But you didn't tell the truth," said Mark. "You don't have to buy a license."

57

"Oh, what's the odds?" said Ben, whose ideas on the subject of truth were far from being strict. "It's all fair in business. Didn't that chap open his eyes when I told him about paying five hundred dollars?"

"I don't think it's right, Ben," said Mark seriously.

"Don't you go preaching, Mark," said Ben, not altogether pleased. "You've been tied to an old woman's apron string too long -- that's what's the matter with you."

"Mother Watson didn't teach me the truth," said Mark. "She didn't care whether I tell it or not except to her. It was my mother that told me I ought always to tell the truth."

"Women don't know anything about business," said Ben. "Nobody in business speaks the truth. Do you see that sign?"

Mark looked across the street and saw a large placard setting forth that a stock of books and stationery was selling off at less than cost.

"Do you believe that?" asked Ben.

"Perhaps it's true," said Mark.

"Then you're jolly green, that's all I've got to say," said Ben. "But you haven't told me how much you've made."

"See here," said Mark, and he drew out his stock of money.

"Whew!" whistled Ben in amazement. "You're in luck. I guess you've been speculatin' on your license too."

"No," said Mark. "One gentleman gave me fifty cents, and two others paid me double price."

"Why, you're gettin' rich!" said Ben. "Ain't you glad you've left the old woman?"

But just then Mark lifted up his eyes and saw a sight that blanched his cheek. There, bearing down upon him and already but a few feet distant, was Mother Watson! She was getting over the ground as fast as her stoutness would allow. She had already caught sight of Mark, and her inflamed eyes were sparkling with triumphant joy. Mark saw with terror that her hand was already feeling in her pocket where she kept the leather strap. Much as he always feared the strap, the idea of having it applied to him in the public streets made it even more distasteful.

"What shall I do, Ben?" he said clutching the arm of his companion.

"What are you afraid of? Do you see a cop after you?"

A "cop" is a street-boy's name for a policeman.

"No," said Mark. "There's Mother Watson coming after me. Don't you see her?"

"That's Mother Watson, is it?" asked Ben, surveying the old body with a critical eye. "She's a beauty, she is!"

"What shall I do, Ben? She'll beat me."

"No, she won't," said Ben. "You just keep quiet, and leave her to me. Don't be afraid. She shan't touch you."

"She might strike you," said Mark apprehensively.

"She'd better not!" said Ben very decidedly. "Not unless she wants to be landed in the middle of next week at very short notice."

By this time Mother Watson came up, puffing and panting with the extraordinary efforts she had made. She could not speak at first but stood and glared at the match boy in a vindictive way.

"What's the matter with you, old lady?" asked Ben coolly. "You ain't sick, be you? I'd offer to support your delicate form, but I'm afraid you'd be too much for me."

"What do you mean by runnin' away from home, you little thief?" said the old woman, at length regaining her breath. Of course her remark was addressed to Mark.

"You're very polite, old lady," said Ben, "but I've adopted that boy, and he's goin' to live with me now."

"I ain't speakin' to you, you vagabond!" said Mother Watson, "so you needn't give me no more of your impertinence. I'm speakin' to him."

"I'm not going to live with you anymore," said Mark, gaining a little courage from the coolness of his friend, the bootblack.

"Ain't a goin' to live with me?" gasped the old woman, who could hardly believe she heard right. "Come right away, sir, or I shall drag you home."

"Don't you stir, Mark," said Ben.

Mother Watson drew out her strap and tried to get at the match boy, but Ben put himself persistently in her way.

"Clear out, you vagabond!" said the old lady, "or I'll give you something to make you quiet."

"You'd better keep quiet yourself," said Ben, not in the least frightened. "Don't you be afraid, Mark. If she kicks up a rumpus, I'll give her over to a cop. He'll settle her."

Mother Watson by this time was very much incensed. She pulled out her strap and tried to get at Mark, but the bootblack foiled her efforts constantly.

59

Carried away with anger, she struck Ben with the strap.

"Look here, old lady," said Ben, "that's goin' a little too far. You won't use that strap again," and with a dexterous and vigorous grasp he pulled it out of her hand.

"Give me that strap, you vagabond!" screamed the old woman furiously.

"Look here, old lady, what are you up to?" demanded the voice of one having authority.

Mother Watson, turning round, saw an object for which she had never had much partiality -- a policeman.

"Oh sir," said she bursting into maudlin tears, "it's my bad boy that I want to come home, and he won't come."

"Which is your boy -- that one?" asked the policeman pointing to Ben Gibson.

"No, not that vagabond!" said the old woman spitefully. "I wouldn't own him. It's the other boy."

"Do you belong to her?" asked the officer addressing Mark.

"No, sir," said the match boy.

"He does," vociferated the old woman.

"Is he your son?"

"No," she said after a moment's hesitation.

"Is he any relation of yours?"

"Yes, he's my nephew," said Mother Watson, making up her mind to a falsehood as the only means of recovering Mark.

"Is this true?" asked the officer.

"No, it isn't," said Mark. "She's no relation to me, but when my mother died she offered to take care of me. Instead of that she's half starved me, and beaten me with a strap when I didn't bring home as much money as she wanted.

"Then you don't want to go back with her?"

"No, I'm going to take care of myself."

"Is there anybody that will prove the truth of what you say?"

"Yes," said Mark. "I'll call Mrs. Flanagan."

"Who is she?"

"She lives in the same house with us."

"Shall he call her, or will you give him up?" asked the officer. "By the way, I think you're the same woman I saw drunk in the street last week."

Mother Watson took alarm at this remark and muttering that it was hard upon a poor widowed woman to take her only nephew from her, she shuffled off, leaving Mark and Ben in full possession of the field, with the terrible strap thrown in as a trophy of the victory they had won.

"I know her of old," said the policeman. "I guess you'll do as well without her as with her."

Satisfied that there would be no more trouble, he resumed his walk, and Mark felt that now in truth he was free and independent.

As Mother Watson will not reappear in this story, it may be said that only a fortnight later she was arrested for an assault upon her sister, the proprietor of the apple stand, from whom she had endeavored in vain to extort a loan, and was sentenced to the Island for a period of three months, during which she ceased to grace metropolitan society.

CHAPTER XII

THE NEWSBOYS' LODGING HOUSE

When Mother Watson had turned the corner, Mark breathed a sigh of relief.

"Don't you think she'll come back again?" he asked anxiously of Ben Gibson.

"No," said Ben, "she's scared of the cop. If she ever catches you alone and tries to come any of her games, just call a cop, and she'll be in a hurry to leave."

"Well," said Mark, "I guess I'll try to sell the rest of my matches. I haven't got but a few."

"All right, I'll try for another shine, and then we'll go and have some lunch. I'd like to get hold of another greeny."

Mark started with his few remaining matches. The feeling that he was his own master and had a little hoard of money for present expenses gave him courage, and he was no longer deterred by his usual timidity. In an hour he had succeeded in getting rid of all his matches, and he was now the possessor of two dollars and seventy-five cents, including the money Ben Gibson owed him. Ben also was lucky enough to get two ten-cent customers, which helped his receipts by twenty cents. Ben, it may be remarked, was not an advocate of the one-price system. He blacked boots for five cents when he could get no more. When he thought there was a reasonable prospect of getting ten cents, that was his price. Sometimes, as in the case of the young man from the rural districts, he advanced his fee to twenty-five cents. I don't approve of Ben's system for my part. I think it savors considerably of sharp practice, and that fair prices in the long run are the best for all parties.

The boys met again at one o'clock, and adjourned to a cheap underground restaurant on Nassau Street where they obtained what seemed to them a luxurious meal of beefsteak with a potato, a small plate of bread, and a cup of what went by the name of coffee. The steak was not quite up to the same article at Delmonico's, and there might be some reasonable doubts as to whether the coffee was a genuine article, but as neither of the boys knew the difference, we may quote Ben's familiar phrase, and say, "What's the odds?"

Indeed the free and easy manner in which Ben threw himself back in his chair, and the condescending manner in which he assured the waiter that the steak was "a prime article," could hardly have been surpassed in the most aristocratic circles.

"Well, Mark, have you had enough?" asked Ben.

"Yes," said Mark.

"Well, I haven't," said Ben. "I guess I'll have some puddin'. Look here, Johnny," to the waiter, "just bring a feller a plate of apple pie with both kinds of sauce."

After giving this liberal order Ben tilted his chair back and began to pick his teeth with his fork. He devoted himself with assiduity to the consumption of the pudding and concluded his expensive repast by the purchase of a two-cent cigar, with which he ascended to the street.

"Better have a cigar, Mark," he said.

"No, thank you," said the match boy. "I think I'd rather not."

"Oh, you're feared of being sick. You'll come to it in time. All business men smoke."

"Bring a feller a plate of apple pie ... "

It is unnecessary to dwell upon the events of the afternoon. Mark was satisfied with the result of his morning's work, and he waited about with Ben till the close of the afternoon when the question came up as to where the boys might sleep for the night.

"I guess we'd better go to the Lodge," said Ben. "Were you ever there?"

"No," said Mark.

"Well, come along. They'll give us a jolly bed, all for six cents, and there's a good, warm room to stay in. Then we can get breakfast in the mornin' for six cents more."

"All right," said Mark. "We'll go."

The downtown Newsboys' Lodging House was at that time located at the corner of Fulton and Nassau Streets. It occupied the fifth and sixth stories of the building then known as the Sun building, owned by Moses S. Beach, the publisher of that journal. In the year 1868 circumstances rendered it expedient to remove the Lodge to a building in Park Place. It is to be hoped that some day not far distant the Children's Aid Society, who carry on this beneficent institution, will be able to erect a building of their own in some eligible locality, which can be permanently devoted to a purpose so praiseworthy.

Ben and Mark soon reached the entrance to the Lodge on Fulton Street. They ascended several flights of narrow stairs till they reached the top story. Then, opening a door at the left, they found themselves in the main room of the Lodge. It was a low-studded room of considerable dimensions amply supplied with windows looking out on Fulton and Nassau Streets. At the side nearest the door was a low platform, separated from the rest of the room by a railing. On this platform were a table and two or three chairs. This was the place for the superintendent, and for gentlemen who from time to time addressed the boys.

The superintendent was at that time Mr. Charles O'Connor, who still retains the office. Probably no one could be found better adapted to the difficult task of managing the class of boys who avail themselves of the good offices of the Newsboys' Home. His mild yet firm manner, and more than all the conviction that he is their friend and feels a hearty interest in their welfare, secure a degree of decorum and good behavior which could hardly be anticipated. Oaths and vulgar speech, however common in the street, are rarely heard here, or, if heard, meet with instant rebuke.

The superintendent was in the room when Ben and Mark entered.

"Well, Ben, what luck have you had today?" said Mr. O'Connor.

"Pretty good," said Ben.

"And who is that with you?"

"Mother Watson's nephew," said Ben with a grimace.

"He's only joking, sir," said Mark. "My name is Mark Manton."

"I am glad to see you, Mark," said the superintendent. "What is your business?"

"I sell matches, sir."

"Have you parents living?"

"No, sir. They are both dead."

"Where have you been living?"

"In Vandewater Street."

"With any one?"

"Yes, with a woman they call Mother Watson."

"Is she a relation of yours?"

"No, sir," said Mark hastily.

"What sort of woman is she?"

"Bad enough, sir. She gets drunk about every day and used to beat me with a strap when I did not bring home as much money as she expected."

"So you have left her?"

"Yes, sir."

"Have you ever been up here before?"

"No, sir."

"I suppose you know the rules of the place."

"Yes, sir. Ben has told me."

"You had better go and wash. We shall have supper pretty quick. Have you any money?"

"Yes, sir."

Mark took out his hoard of money and showed it to the superintendent, who was surprised at the amount.

"How did you get so much?" he asked.

"Part of it was given to me," said Mark.

"What are you going to do with it? You don't need it all?"

"Will you keep it for me, sir?"

"I will put as much of it as you can spare into the bank for you. This is our bank."

He pointed to a table beside the railing on the outside. The top of it was pierced with narrow slits, each having a number attached. Each compartment was assigned to any boy who desired it, and his daily earnings were dropped in at the end of the day. Once a month the bank was opened, and the depositor was at liberty to withdraw his savings if he desired it. This is an excellent arrangement, as it has a tendency to teach frugal habits to the young patrons of the Lodge. Extravagance is one of their besetting sins. Many average a dollar and over as daily earnings, yet are always ragged and out at the elbows, and often are unsupplied with the small price of a night's lodging at the Home. The money is squandered on gambling, cigars, and theater-going, while the same sum would make them comfortable and independent of charity. The disposition to save is generally the first encouraging symptom in a street boy and shows that he really has a desire to rise above his circumstances and gain a respectable position in the world.

Ben, who had long frequented the Lodging House off and on, led the way to the washing room, where Mark, to his satisfaction, was able to cleanse himself from the dust and impurity of the street. At Mother Watson's he had had no accommodations of the kind, as the old lady was not partial to water either internally or externally. He was forced to snatch such opportunities as he could find.

The washroom at the Newsboys Lodging House, May 1867

"Now," said Ben, "we'll go into the gymnasium."

A room opposite the main room had been fitted up with a few of the principal appliances of a gymnasium, and these were already in use by quite a number of boys.

Mark looked on but did not participate, partly from bashfulness and partly because he did not very well understand the use of the different appliances.

"How do you like it?" asked Ben.

"Very much," said Mark with satisfaction. "I'm glad you brought me here."

"I'll show you the beds by and by," said Ben.

The room on the floor below was used for lodging. Tiers of neat beds, some like those on a steamboat or a hospital, filled a large room. They were very neat in appearance and looked comfortable. In order to insure their continuing neatness, the superintendent requires those who need it to wash their feet before retiring to bed.

"THE LARGE, AIRY DORMITORY, CLEAN AS A SHIP'S DECK, WITH WIRE-BEDS ARRANGED ON IRON FRAMES."

St. Nicholas Magazine printed this sketch of a "large, airy dormitory, clean as a ship's deck, with wire-beds arranged on iron frames" at a Children's Aid Society boys' lodging house in New York City in the second half of the nineteenth century.

The supper was of course plain but of good quality and sufficient quantity.

About nine o'clock Mark got into the neat bed which was assigned to him and felt that it was more satisfactory even than the cabin of a Brooklyn ferryboat. He slept peacefully except towards morning, when he dreamed that his ole persecutor, Mother Watson, was about to apply the dreaded strap. He woke up terrified but soon realized with deep satisfaction that he was no longer in her clutches.

CHAPTER XIII

WHAT BEFELL THE MATCH BOY

During the next three months Mark made his home at the Lodging House. He was easily able to meet the small charges of the Lodge for bed and breakfast, and he saved up ten dollars besides in the bank. Ben Gibson began to look upon him as quite a capitalist.

"I don't see how you save up so much money, Mark," he said. "You don't earn mor'n half as much as I do."

"It's because you spend so much, Ben. It costs you considerable for cigars and such things, you know, and then you go to the Old Bowery pretty often."

A feller must have some fun," said Ben. "They've got a tearin' play at the Bowery now. You'd better come tonight."

Mark shook his head.

"I feel pretty tired when it comes night," he said. "I'd rather stay at home."

"You ain't so tough as I am," said Ben.

"No," said Mark, "I don't feel very strong. I think something's the matter with me."

"Nothin' ain't ever the matter with me," said Ben complacently, "but you're a puny little chap, that look as if you might blow away some day."

It was now April, and the weather was of the mild character that saps the strength and produces a feeling of weakness and debility. Mark had been exposed during the winter to the severity of stormy weather, and more than once got thoroughly drenched. It was an exposure that Ben would only have laughed at, but Mark was slightly built, without much strength of constitution, and he had been feeling very languid for a few days, so that it was with an effort that he dragged himself round during the day with his little bundle of matches.

This conversation with Ben took place in the morning just as both boys were going to work.

They separated at the City Hall Park, Ben finding a customer in front of the Times building, while Mark, after a little deliberation, decided to go on to Pearl Street with his matches. He had visited the offices in most of the lower streets, but this was a new region to him, and he thought he might meet with better success there. So he kept on his way.

The warm sun and the sluggish air made his head ache, and he felt little disposition to offer his wares for sale. At length he reached a large warehouse with these names displayed on the sign over the door: ROCKWELL & COOPER.

This, as the reader will remember, was the establishment in which Richard Hunter, formerly Ragged Dick, was now bookkeeper.

At this point a sudden faintness came over Mark, and he sank to the ground insensible.

A moment before Richard Hunter handed a couple of letters to the office boy, known to the readers of the earlier volumes in this series as Micky Maguire, and said, "Michael, I should like to have you carry these at once to the post office. On the way you may stop at Trescott & Wayne's, and get this bill cashed, if possible."

"All right, Mr. Hunter," said Michael respectfully.

Richard Hunter and Micky Maguire had been bootblacks together and had had more than one contest for the supremacy. They had been sworn enemies, and Micky had done his utmost to injure Richard, but the latter, by his magnanimity, had finally wholly overcome the antipathy of his former foe and, when opportunity offered, had lifted him to a position in the office where he was himself employed. In return, Micky had become an enthusiastic admirer of Richard, and so far from taking advantage of their former relations, had voluntarily taken up the habit of addressing him as Mr. Hunter.

Michael went out on his errand but just outside the door came near stepping on the prostrate form of the little match boy.

"Get up here!" he said roughly, supposing at first that Mark had thrown himself down out of laziness and gone to sleep.

Mark didn't answer, and Micky, bending over, saw his fixed expression and waxen pallor.

"Maybe the little chap's dead," he thought, startled, and, without more ado, took him up in his strong arms and carried him into the counting room.

"Who have you got there, Michael?" asked Richard Hunter turning round in surprise.

"A little match boy that was lyin' just outside the door. He looks as if he might be dead."

Richard jumped at once from his stool and, approaching the boy, looked earnestly in his face.

"He has fainted away," he said after a pause. "Bring some water, quick!"

Micky brought a glass of water, which was thrown in the face of Mark. The match boy gave a little shiver and, opening his eyes, fixed them upon Richard Hunter.

"Where am I?" he asked vacantly.

"You are with friends," said Richard gently. "You were found at our door faint. Do you feel sick?"

"I feel weak," said Mark.

"Have you been well lately?"

"No, I've felt tired and weak."

"Are you a match boy?"

"Yes."

"Have you parents living?"

"No," said Mark.

"Poor fellow!" said Richard. "I know how to pity you. I have no parents either."

"But you have got money," said Mark. "You don't have to live in the street."

"I was once a street boy like you."

"You!" repeated the match boy in surprise.

"Yes. But where do you sleep?"

"At the Lodging House."

"It is a good place. Michael, you had better go to the post office now."

Mark looked about him a little anxiously.

"Where are my matches?" he asked.

"Just outside. I'll get them," said Michael promptly.

He brought them in and then departed on his errand.

"I guess I'd better be going," said Mark rising feebly.

"No," said Richard. "You are not able. Come here and sit down. You will feel stronger by and by. Did you eat any breakfast this morning?"

"A little," said Mark, "but I was not very hungry."

"Do you think you could eat anything now?"

Mark shook his head.

"No," he said, "I don't feel hungry. I only feel tired."

"Would you like to rest?"

"Yes. That's all I want."

"Come here then, and I will see what I can do for you."

Mark followed his new friend into the warehouse where Richard found a soft bale of cotton and told Mark he might lie down upon it. This the poor boy was glad enough to do. In his weakness he was disposed to sleep and soon closed his eyes in slumber. Several times Richard went out to look at him but found him dozing and was unwilling to interrupt him.

The day wore away, and afternoon came.

Mark got up from his cotton bale and with unsteady steps came to the door of the counting room.

"I'm going," he said.

Richard turned round.

"Where are you going?"

"I'm going to the Lodge. I think I won't sell any more matches today."

"I'll take all you've left," said Richard. "Don't trouble yourself about them. But you are not going to the Lodge."

Mark looked at him in surprise.

"I shall take you home with me tonight," he said. "You are not well, and I will look after you. At the Lodge there will be a crowd of boys, and the noise will do you harm."

"You are very kind," said Mark, "but I'm afraid I'll trouble you."

"No," said Richard, "I shan't count it a trouble. I was once a poor boy like you and found friends. I'll be your friend. Go back and lie down again, and in about an hour I shall be ready to take you with me."

It seemed strange to Mark to think that there was somebody who proposed to protect and look after him. In many of the offices which he visited he was met with rough treatment and was ordered out of the way, as if he were a dog and without human feelings. Many who treated him this way were really kind-hearted men who had at home children whom they loved, but they appeared to forget that these neglected children of the street had feelings and wants as well as their own children, who were tenderly nurtured. They did not remember that they were somebody's children, and that cold and harshness and want were as hard for them to bear as for those in a higher rank of life. But Mark was in that state of weakness when it seemed sweet to throw off all care or thought for the future and to sink back upon the soft bale with the thought that he had nothing to do but to rest.

"That boy is going to be sick," thought Richard Hunter to himself. "I think he is going to have a fever."

It was because of this thought that he decided to carry him home. He had a kind heart, and he knew how terrible a thing sickness is to these little street waifs who have no mother or sister to smooth their pillow or cheer them with gentle words. The friendless condition of the little match boy touched his heart, and he resolved that as he had the means of taking care of him he would do so.

"Michael," he said at the close of business hours, "I wish you would call a cab."

"What, to come here?" asked Micky surprised.

"Yes. I am going to take that little boy home with me. I think he is going to be sick, and I am afraid he would have a hard time of it if I sent him back into the street."

"Bully for you, Mr. Hunter!" said Micky, who, though rough in his outward manners, was yet capable of appreciating kindness in others. There were times indeed in the past when he had treated smaller boys brutally, but it was under the influence of passion. He had improved greatly since, and his better nature was beginning to show itself.

Micky calls a handsome cab for Richard and Mark.

Micky went out and soon returned in state inside a cab. He was leaning back thinking it would be a very good thing if he had a carriage of his own to ride in. But I am afraid that day will never come. Micky has already turned out much better than was expected, but he is hardly likely to rise much higher than the subordinate position he now occupies. In capacity and education he is far inferior to his old associate, Richard Hunter, who is destined to rise much higher than at present.

Richard Hunter went to the rear of the warehouse where Mark still lay on his bale.

"Come," he said, "we'll go home now."

Mark rose from his recumbent position, and walked to the door. He saw with surprise the carriage, the door of which Micky Maguire held open.

"Are we going to ride in that?" he asked.

"Yes," said Richard Hunter. "Let me help you in."

The little match boy sank back in the soft seat in vague surprise at his good luck. He could not help wondering what Ben Gibson would say if he could see him now.

Richard Hunter sat beside him and supported Mark's head. The driver whipped up his horse, and they were speedily on their way up the Bowery to St. Mark's Place.

CHAPTER XIV

RICHARD HUNTER'S WARD

It was half-past five o'clock in the afternoon when the carriage containing Richard Hunter and the match boy stopped in front of his boarding place in St. Mark's Place. Richard helped the little boy out, saying cheerfully, "Well, we've got home."

"Is this where you live?" asked Mark faintly.

"Yes. How do you like it?"

"It's a nice place. I am afraid you are taking too much trouble about me."

"Don't think of that. Come in."

Richard had ascended the front steps after paying the carriage driver and, taking out his night key, opened the outside door.

"Come upstairs," he said.

They ascended two flights of stairs, and Richard threw open the door of his room. A fire was already burning in the grate, and it looked bright and cheerful.

"Do you feel tired?" asked Richard.

"Yes, a little."

"Then lie right down in the bed. You are hungry too, are you not?"

"A little."

"I will have something sent up to you."

Just then Fosdick -- who, it will be remembered, was Richard Hunter's roommate -- entered the room. He looked with surprise at Mark, and then inquiringly at Richard.

"It is a little match boy," explained the latter, "who fell in a fainting fit in front of our office. I think the poor fellow is going to be sick, so I brought him home and mean to take care of him till he is well."

"You must let me share the expense, Dick," said Fosdick

"No, but I'll let you take care of him. That will do just as well."

"But I would rather share the expense. He reminds me of the way I was situated when I fell in with you. What is your name?"

"Mark Manton," said the match boy.

"I've certainly seen him somewhere before," said Fosdick reflectively. "His face looks familiar to me."

"So it does to me. Perhaps I've seen him about the streets somewhere."

"I have it," said Fosdick suddenly. "Don't you remember the boy we saw sleeping in the cabin of the Fulton ferryboat?"

"Yes."

"I think he is the one. Mark," he continued, turning to the match boy, "didn't you sleep one night in a Brooklyn ferryboat about three months ago?"

"Yes," said Mark.

"And did you find anything in your vest pocket in the morning?"

"Yes," said the match boy with interest. "I found a dollar and didn't know where it came from. Was it you that put it in?"

"He had a hand in it," said Fosdick pointing with a smile to his roommate.

"I was very glad to get it," said Mark. "I only had eight cents besides, and that gave me enough to buy some matches. That was at the time I ran away."

"Who did you run away from?"

"From Mother Watson."

"Mother Watson?" repeated Dick. "I wonder if I don't know her. She is a very handsome old lady, with a fine red complexion, particularly around the nose."

"Yes," said Mark with a smile.

"And she takes whiskey when she can get it?"

"Yes."

"How did you fall in with her?"

"She promised to take care of me when my mother died, but instead of that she wanted me to earn money for her."

"Yes, she was always a very disinterested old lady. So it appears you didn't like her as a guardian?"

"No."

"Then suppose you take me. Would you like to be my ward?"

"I think I would, but I don't know what it means," said Mark.

"It means that I'm to look after you," said Dick, "just as if I was your uncle or grandfather. You may call me grandfather if you want to."

"Oh, you're too young," said Mark, amused in spite of his weakness.

"Then we won't decide just at present about the name. But I forgot all about your being hungry."

"I'm not very hungry."

"At any rate, you haven't had anything to eat since morning and need something. I'll go down and see Mrs. Wilson about it."

Richard Hunter soon explained matters to Mrs. Wilson, to whom he offered to pay an extra weekly sum for Mark, and arranged that a small single bed should be placed in one corner of the room temporarily in which the match boy should sleep. He speedily reappeared with a bowl of broth, a cup of tea and some dry toast. The sight of these caused the match boy's eyes to brighten, and he was able to do very good justice to all.

"Now," said Richard Hunter, "I will call in a doctor and find out what is the matter with my little ward."

In the course of the evening Dr. Pemberton, a young dispensary physician whose acquaintance Richard had casually made, called at his request and looked at the patient.

"He is not seriously sick," he pronounced. "It is chiefly debility that troubles him, brought on probably by exposure and over-exertion in this languid weather."

"Then you don't think he is going to have a fever?" said Dick.

"No, not if he remains under your care. If he had continued in the street, I think he would not have escaped one."

"What shall we do for him?"

"Rest is most important of all. That, with nourishing food and freedom from exposure, will soon bring him round again."

"He shall have all these."

"I suppose you know him, as you take so much interest in him?"

"No, I never saw him but once before today, but I am able to befriend him, and he has no other friends."

"There are not many young men who would take all this trouble about a poor match boy," said the doctor.

"It's because they don't know how hard it is to be friendless and neglected," said Dick. "I've known that feeling, and it makes me pity those who are in the same condition I once was."

"I wish there were more like you, Mr. Hunter," said Dr. Pemberton. "There would be less suffering in the world. As to our patient here, I have no doubt he will do well and soon be on his legs again."

Indeed Mark was already looking better and feeling better. The rest which he had obtained during the day, and the refreshment he had just taken were precisely what he needed. He soon fell asleep, and Richard and Fosdick, lighting the gas lamp on the center table, sat down to their evening studies.

In a few days Mark was decidedly better, but it was thought best that he should still keep the room. He liked it very well in the evening when Dick and Fosdick were at home, but he felt rather lonesome in the daytime. Richard Hunter thought of this one day and said, "Can you read, Mark?"

"Yes," said the match boy.

"Who taught you? Not Mother Watson, surely."

"No, she couldn't read herself. It was my mother who taught me."

"I think I must get you two or three books of stories to read while we are away in the daytime."

"You are spending too much money for me, Mr. Hunter."

"Remember I am your guardian, and it is my duty to take care of you."

The next morning on his way downtown, Richard Hunter stepped into a retail bookstore on Broadway. As he entered, a boy, if indeed it be allowed to apply such a term to a personage so consequential in his manners, came forward.

"What, Roswell Crawford, are you here?" asked Richard Hunter in surprise.

Roswell, who has already been mentioned in this story and who figured considerably in previous volumes of this series, answered rather stiffly to this salutation.

"Yes," he said. "I am here for a short time. I came in to oblige Mr. Baker."

"You were always very obliging, Roswell," said Richard good-humoredly.

Roswell did not appear to appreciate this compliment. He probably thought it savored of irony.

"Do you want to buy anything this morning?" he said shortly.

"Yes, I would like to look at some books of fairy stories."

"For your own reading, I suppose," said Roswell.

"I may read them, but I am getting them for my ward."

"Is he a bootblack?" sneered Roswell, who knew all about Dick's early career.

"No," said Richard, "he's a match boy, so if you've got any books that you can warrant to be just the thing for match boy, I should like to see them."

"We don't have many customers of that class," said Roswell unpleasantly. "They generally go to cheaper establishments, when they are able to read."

"Do they?" said Dick. "I'm glad you've got into a job where you only meet the cream of society," and Dick glanced significantly at a red-nosed man who came in to buy a couple sheets of notepaper.

Roswell colored.

"There are some exceptions," he said and glanced pointedly at Richard Hunter himself.

"Well," said Dick, after looking over a collection of juvenile books, "I'll take these two."

He drew out his pocketbook and handed Roswell a ten-dollar bill. Roswell changed it with a feeling of jealousy and envy. He was the "son of a gentleman," as he often boasted, but he had never had a ten-dollar bill in his pocket. Indeed, he was now working for six dollars a week and glad to get that after having been out of work for several months.

Just then Mr. Gladden, of the large downtown firm of Gladden & Co., came into the store and, seeing Richard, saluted him cordially.

"How are you this morning, Mr. Hunter?" he said. "Are you on your way downtown?"

"Yes, sir," said Richard.

"Come with me. We will take the omnibus together," and the two walked out of the store in familiar conversation.

"I shouldn't think that such a man as Mr. Gladden would notice a low bootblack," said Roswell bitterly.

The rest of the day he was made unhappy by the thought of Dick's prosperity and his own hard fate in being merely a clerk in a bookstore with a salary of six dollars a week.

CHAPTER XV

MARK GETS A JOB

In a week from the purchase of the books, Mark felt that he was fully recovered. He never had much color, but the unhealthy pallor had left his cheeks, and he had an excellent appetite.

"Well, Mark, how do you feel tonight?" asked Richard on his return from the store one evening.

"I'm all right, now, Mr. Hunter. I think I will go to work, tomorrow morning."

"What sort of work?"

Selling matches."

"Do you like to sell matches?"

"I like it better than selling papers or blacking boots."

"But wouldn't you like better to be in a store?"

"I couldn't get a job," said Mark.

"Why not?"

"My clothes are ragged," said the match boy with some hesitation. "Besides I haven't got anybody to refer to."

"Can't you refer to your guardian?" asked Richard Hunter smiling.

"Do you think I had better try to get a place in a store, Mr. Hunter?" asked Mark.

"Yes, I think it would be much better for you than to sell matches in the street. You are not a strong boy, and the exposure is not good for you. As to your clothes, we'll see if we cannot supply you with something better than you have on."

"But," said Mark. "I want to pay for my clothes myself. I have got ten dollars in the bank at the Newsboys' Lodge."

"Very well. You can go down tomorrow morning and get it. But we needn't wait for that. I will go and get you some clothes before I go to business."

In the morning Richard Hunter went out with the match boy and, for twenty dollars, obtained for him a very neat gray suit, besides a supply of under-clothing. Mark put them on at once and felt not a little pleased with the improvement in his appearance.

"You can carry your old clothes to Mr. O'Connor," said Richard. "They are not very good, but they are better than none, and he may have the opportunity of giving them away."

"You have been very kind to me, Mr. Hunter," said Mark gratefully. "Goodbye."

"Goodbye? What makes you say that?"

"Because I am going now to the Newsboys' Lodge."

"Yes, but you are coming back again."

"But I think I had better go there to live now. It will be much cheaper, and I ought not to put you to so much expense."

"You're a good boy, Mark, but you must remember that I am your guardian and am to be obeyed as such. You're not going back to the Lodge to live. I have arranged to have you stay with me at my boarding place. As soon as you have got a job you will work in the daytime, and every Saturday night you will bring me your money. In the evening I shall have you study a little, for I don't want you to grow up as ignorant as I was at your age."

"Were you ignorant, Mr. Hunter?" asked Mark with interest.

"Yes, I was," said Richard. "When I was fourteen, I couldn't read nor write."

"I can hardly believe that, Mr. Hunter," said Mark. "You're such a fine scholar."

"Am I?" asked Richard smiling yet well pleased with the compliment.

"Why, you can read French as fast as I can read English and write beautifully."

"Well, I had to work hard to do it," said Richard Hunter. "But I feel paid for all the time I've spent in trying to improve myself. Sometimes I've thought I should like to spend the evening at some place of amusement rather than study, but if I had, there'd be nothing to show for it now. Take my advice, Mark, and study all you can, and you'll grow up respectable and respected."

"Now," he added after a pause, "I'll tell you what you may do. You may look in my Herald every morning and whenever you see a boy advertised for, you can call, or whenever, in going along the street, you see a notice 'Boy wanted,' you may call in, and sooner or later you'll get something. If they ask for references, you may refer to Richard Hunter, bookkeeper for Rockwell & Cooper."

"Thank you, Mr. Hunter," said Mark. "I will do so."

On parting with his guardian the match boy went downtown to the Lodging House. The superintendent received him kindly.

"I didn't know what had become of you, Mark," he said. "If it had been some of the boys, I should have been afraid they had got into a scrape and gone to the Island. But I didn't think that of you."

"I hope you'll never hear that of me, Mr. O'Connor," said Mark.

"I hope not. I'm always sorry to hear of any boy's going astray. But you seem to have been doing well since I saw you," and the superintendent glanced at Mark's new clothes.

"I've met with some kind friends," said the match boy. "I have been sick, and they took care of me."

"And now you have come back to the Lodge."

"Yes, but not to stay. I came for the money that I have saved up in the bank. It is going for these clothes."

"Very well. You shall have it. What is the name of the friend who has taken care of you?"

"Richard Hunter."

"I know him," said the superintendent. "He is an excellent young man. You could not be in better hands."

On leaving the Lodge, Mark felt a desire to find his old ally, Ben Gibson, who, though rather a tough character, had been kind to him.

Ben was not difficult to find. During business hours he was generally posted on Nassau Street, somewhere between Fulton Street and Spruce Street.

He was just polishing off a customer's boots when Mark came up and touched him lightly on the shoulder. Ben looked up, but did not at first recognize the match boy in the neatly dressed figure before him.

"Shine yer boots!" he asked in a professional tone.

"Why, Ben, don't you know me?" asked Mark laughing.

"My eyes, if it ain't Mark, the match boy!" exclaimed Ben in surprise. "Where've you been all this while, Mark?"

"I've been sick, Ben."

"I'd like to be sick too, if that's the way you got them clo'es. I didn't know what had 'come of you."

"I found some good friends," said Mark.

If your friends have got any more good clo'es they want to get rid of," said Ben, "tell 'em you know a chap that can take care of a few. Are you in the match business now?"

"I haven't been doing anything for three weeks," said Mark.

"Goin' to sell matches again?"

"No."

"Sellin' papers?"

"No, I'm trying to find a job in a store."

"I don't think I'd like to be in a store," said Ben reflectively. "I'm afraid my delicate constitution couldn't stand the confinement. Besides, I'm my own boss now and don't have nobody to order me around."

"But you don't expect to black boots all your life, Ben, do you?"

"I dunno," said Ben. "Maybe when I'm married, I'll choose some other business. It would be rather hard to support a family at five cents a shine. Are you comin' to the Lodge tonight?"

"No," said Mark, "I'm boarding up at St. Mark's Place."

"Mother Watson hasn't opened a fashionable boardin' house up there, has she?"

"I guess not," said Mark smiling. "I can't think of what has become of her. I haven't seen her since the day she tried to carry me off."

"I've heard of her," said Ben. "She's stoppin' with some friends at the Island. They won't let her come away on account of likin' her company so much."

"I hope I shall never see her again," said Mark with a shudder. "She is a wicked old woman. But I must be going, Ben."

"I s'pose you'll come and see a feller now and then."

"Yes, Ben, when I get time. But I hope to get a job soon."

Mark walked leisurely up Broadway. Having been confined to the house for three weeks, he enjoyed the excitement of being out in the street once more. The shop windows looked brighter and merrier than before, and the little match boy felt that the world was a very pleasant place after all.

He had passed Eighth Street before he was fairly aware of the distance he had traversed. He found himself looking into the window of a bookstore. While examining the articles in the window his eye suddenly caught the notice pasted in the middle of the glass on a piece of white paper: BOY WANTED.

"Perhaps they'll take me," thought Mark suddenly. "At any rate I'll go in see."

Accordingly he entered the store and looked about him a little undecidedly.

"Well, sonny, what do you want?" asked the clerk.

I see that you want a boy," said Mark.

83

"Yes. Do you want a job?"

"I am trying to get one."

"Well, go and see that gentleman about it."

He pointed to a gentleman who was seated at a desk in the corner of the store.

"Please, sir, do you want a boy?" he asked.

"Yes," said the gentleman. "How old are you?"

"Ten years old."

"You are rather young. Have you worked in a store before?"

"No, sir."

"Do you know your way about the city pretty well?"

"Yes, sir."

"I want a boy to deliver papers and magazines and carry small parcels of books. Do you think you could do that?"

"Yes, sir."

"Without stopping to play on the way?"

"Yes, sir."

"I have just discharged one boy because he was gone an hour and a half on an errand to Twentieth Street. You are the first boy that has answered my advertisement. I'll try you on a salary of three dollars a week, if you can go to work at once. What is your name?"

"Mark Manton."

"Very well, Mark. Go to Mr. Jones, behind the counter there, and he will give you a parcel to carry to West Twenty-first Street."

"I'm in luck," thought Mark. "I didn't expect to get a job so easily."

CHAPTER XVI

MARK'S FIRST IMPRESSIONS

Probably my readers already understand that the bookstore in which Mark has secured a job is the same in which Roswell Crawford is employed. This circumstance, if Mark had only known it, was likely to make his job considerably less desirable than it would otherwise have been. Mr. Baker, the proprietor of the store, was very considerate in his treatment of those in his employ, and Mr. Jones, his chief clerk, was good-natured and pleasant. But Roswell was very apt to be insolent and disagreeable to those who were, or whom he considered to be, in an inferior position to himself, while his lofty ideas of his own dignity and social position as the "son of a gentleman" made him not very agreeable as a clerk. Still he had learned something from his bad luck thus far. He had been so long in getting his present job, that he felt it prudent to sacrifice his pride to some extent for the sake of retaining it. But if he could neglect his duties without attracting attention, he resolved to do it, feeling that six dollars was a beggarly salary for a young gentleman of his position and capacity. It was unfortunate for him, and a source of considerable annoyance, that he could get no one except his mother to assent to his own estimate of his abilities. Even his cousin Gilbert, who had been Rockwell & Cooper's bookkeeper before Richard Hunter succeeded to the position, did not conceal his poor opinion of Roswell; but this the later attributed to prejudice, being persuaded in his own mind that his cousin was somewhat inclined to be envious of his superior abilities.

At the time that Mark was so suddenly engaged by Mr. Baker, Roswell had gone out to lunch. When he returned, Mark had gone out with the parcel to West Twenty-first Street. So they missed each other just at first.

"Well, Crawford," said Mr. Jones as Roswell reentered the store, "Mr. Baker has engaged a new boy."

"Has he? What sort of fellow is he?"

"A little fellow. He doesn't look as if he was more than ten years old."

"Where is he?"

"Mr. Baker sent him on an errand to Twenty-first Street."

"Humph!" said Roswell a little discontented, "I was going to recommend a friend of mine."

"There may be a chance yet. This boy may not suit."

In about five minutes Mr. Baker and Mr. Jones both went out to lunch. It was the middle of the day, when there is very little business, and it would not be difficult for Roswell to attend to any customers who might call.

As soon as he was alone, Roswell got an interesting book from the shelves, and sitting down in his employer's chair, began to read, though this was against the rules in business hours. To see this pompous air with which Roswell threw himself back in his chair, it might have been supposed that he was the proprietor of the establishment, though I believe it is true, as a general rule, that employers are not in the habit of putting on so many airs, unless the position is a new one and they have not yet got over the new feeling of importance which it is apt to inspire at first.

While Roswell was thus engaged Mark returned from his errand.

He looked about him in some uncertainty in entering the store, not seeing Mr. Baker or the chief clerk.

"Come here," said Roswell in a tone of authority.

Mark walked up to the desk.

"So you are the new boy?" said Roswell after a close scrutiny.

"Yes."

"It would be a little more polite to say 'Yes sir.'"

"Yes, sir."

"What is your age?"

"Ten years."

"Humph! You are rather young. If I had been consulted I should have said 'Get a boy of twelve years old.'"

"I hope I shall suit," said Mark.

"I hope so," said Roswell patronizingly. "You will find us very easy to get along with if you do your duty. We were obliged to send away a boy this morning because he played instead of going on his errands at once."

Mark could not help wondering what was Roswell's position in the establishment. He talked as if he were one of the proprietors, but his youthful appearance made it difficult to suppose that.

"What is your name?" continued Roswell.

"Mark Manton."

"Have you worked in any store before?"

"No, sir."

"Do you live with your parents?"

"My parents are dead."

"Then whom do you live with?"

"With my guardian."

"So you have a guardian?" said Roswell a little surprised. "What is his name?"

"Mr. Hunter."

"Hunter!" repeated Roswel hastily. "What is his first name?"

"Richard I believe."

"Dick Hunter!" exclaimed Roswell scornfully. "Do you mean to say that he has charge of you?"

"Yes," said Mark firmly, for he perceived the tone in which his friend was referred to and resented it. Moreover the new expression which came over Roswell's face brought back to his recollection the evening when, for the first time in his life, he had begged in Fulton Market and been scornfully repulsed by Roswell and his mother. Roswell's face had at first seemed familiar to him, but it was only now that he recognized him. Roswell, on the other hand, was not likely to identify the neatly dressed boy before him with the shivering little beggar of the market. But it recurred to him all at once that Dick had referred to his ward as a match boy.

"You were a match boy?" he said, in the manner of one making a grave accusation.

"Yes, sir."

"Then why didn't you keep on selling matches and not try to get a job in a respectable store?"

"Because Mr. Hunter thought it better for me to go into a store."

"Mr. Hunter! Perhaps you didn't know that your guardian, as you call him, used to be a bootblack."

"Yes, he told me so."

"They called him 'Ragged Dick' then," said Roswell turning up his nose. "He couldn't read or write, I believe."

"He's a good scholar now," said Mark.

"Humph! I suppose he told you so. But you mustn't believe all he tells you."

"He wouldn't tell anything but the truth," said Mark, who was bolder on behalf of his friend than he would have been for himself.

"So he did tell you he was a good scholar? I thought so."

"No, he told me nothing about it, but since I have lived with him I've heard him read French as well as English."

"Perhaps that isn't saying much," said Roswell with a sneer. "Can you read yourself?"

"Yes."

"That is more than I expected. What induced Mr. Baker to take a boy from the street is more than I can tell."

"I suppose I can run errands just as well, if I was once a match boy," said Mark, who did not fancy the tone which Roswell assumed towards him and began to doubt whether he was a person of as much importance as he at first supposed.

"We shall see," said Roswell loftily. "But there's one thing I'll advise you, young man, and that is, to treat me with proper respect. You'll find it best to keep friends with me. I can get you turned away at any time."

Mark hardly knew whether to believe this or not. He already began to suspect that Roswell was something of a humbug, and though it was not in his nature to form a causeless dislike, he certainly did not feel disposed to like Roswell. He did not care so much for any slighting remarks upon himself nor for the scorn with which Roswell saw fit to speak of his friend, Richard Hunter, who, by his good offices, had won the little boy's lasting gratitude. Mark did not reply to the threat contained in these last words of Roswell.

"Is there anything for me to do?" he asked.

"Yes, you may dust off those books on the counter. There's the duster hanging up."

This was really Roswell's business, and he ought to have been at work at this instead of reading, but it was characteristic of him to shift his duties upon others. He was not aware of how much time had passed and supposed that Mark would be through before Mr. Baker returned. But that gentleman came in while Roswell was busily engaged in reading.

"Is that the way you do your work, Roswell?" asked his employer.

Roswell jumped to his feet in some confusion.

"I thought I had better set the new boy to work," he said.

"Dusting the books is your work, not his."

"He was doing nothing, sir."

"He will have plenty to do in carrying out parcels. Besides, I don't know that it is any worse for him to be idle than you. You were reading also, which you know is against the rules of the store."

Roswell made no reply, but it hurt his pride considerably to be censured thus in the presence of Mark, to whom he had spoken with such an assumption of power and patronage.

"I wish I had a store of my own," he thought discontentedly. "Then I could do as I pleased without having anybody to interfere with me."

But Roswell did not understand, and there are plenty of boys in the same state of ignorance, that those who fill subordinate positions acceptably are most likely to rise to stations where they will themselves have control over others.

"I suppose you have not been to lunch," said Mr. Baker turning to Mark.

"No, sir."

"You board in St. Mark's Place, I think you said?"

"Yes, sir."

"Very well, here is a parcel to go to East Ninth Street. You may call and leave that at the address marked upon it and may stay out long enough for lunch. But don't be gone more than an hour in all."

"No, sir."

"I'm glad that boy isn't my employer," thought Mark referring of course to Roswell Crawford who, by the way, would have been indignant at such an appellation. "I like Mr. Baker a great deal better."

Mark was punctual to his appointment, and in a little less than an hour reported himself at the store again for duty.

CHAPTER XVII

BAD ADVICE

Roswell pursued his way home with a general sense of discontent. Why should he be so much worse off than Richard Hunter who had only been a ragged bootblack three years before? The whole world seemed to be in conspiracy to advance Richard and to keep him down. To think that he should be only earning six dollars a week while Dick, whom he considered so far beneath him, was receiving twenty was really outrageous. And now he had pushed a low dependent of his into Baker's store where Roswell was obliged to associate with him!

Certainly Roswell's grievances were numerous. But there was one thing he did not understand -- that the greatest obstacle to his advancement was himself. If he had entered any job with the determination to make his services valuable and discharge his duties, whatever they might be, with conscientious fidelity, he would have found his relations with his employer much more agreeable and satisfactory.

Mrs. Crawford still kept the house in Clinton Place, letting nearly all the rooms to lodgers. In this way she succeeded in making both ends meet, though with considerable difficulty, so that she had not the means to supply Roswell with the spending money he desired. Her nephew, James Gilbert, Richard Hunter's predecessor as bookkeeper, still boarded with her. It will be remembered by the readers of "Fame and Fortune" that this Gilbert, on being questioned by Mr. Rockwell as to his share in the plot against Dick, had angrily resigned his position thinking, probably, that he should lose it at any rate.

It so happened that business was generally depressed at this time, and it was three months before he succeeded in obtaining another job, and then he was compelled to work for eight hundred dollars, or two hundred less than he had formerly received. This was a great disappointment to him and did not help his temper much, which had never been very sweet. He felt quite exasperated against Dick, whom, very much against his wishes, had been the means of promoting Dick to his own place. Indeed, on this point, he sympathized heartily with Roswell, whose dislike to Richard Hunter had already been shown.

"Well, mother," said Roswell as he entered Mrs. Crawford's presence, "I'm getting tired of Baker's store."

"Don't say so, Roswell," said his mother in alarm. "Remember how long it took you to get the job."

"I have to work like a dog for six dollars a week," said Roswell.

"Yes," said his cousin with a sneer, "that's precisely the way you work. Dogs spend their time running around the street doing nothing."

"Well, I have to work hard enough," said Roswell, "but I wouldn't mind that so much, if I didn't have to associate with low match boys."

"What do you mean, Roswell?" asked his mother, who did not understand the allusion.

"Baker hired a new boy today, and who do you think he turns out to be?"

"Not that boy, Ragged Dick?"

"No, you don't think he would give up cousin James' job, where he gets a thousand dollars a year, to go into Baker's as a boy?"

"Who was it, then?"

"He used to be a ragged match boy about the street. Dick Hunter picked him up somewhere and got him a job in our store, on purpose to spite me, I expect."

As the reader is aware, Roswell was mistaken in his supposition, as Mark obtained the place on his own responsibility.

"The bootblack seems to be putting on airs," said Mrs. Crawford.

"Yes, he pretends to be the guardian of this match boy."

"What's the boy's name?"

"Mark Manton."

"If I were Mr. Baker," said Mrs. Crawford, "I should be afraid to take a street boy into my employ. Very likely he isn't honest."

"I wish he would steal something," said Roswell not very charitably. "Then we could get rid of him, and the bootblack would be pretty well mortified about it."

"He'll be found out sooner or later," said Mrs. Crawford. "You may depend on that. You'd better keep a sharp lookout for him, Roswell. If you catch him in stealing, it will help you with Mr. Baker, or it ought to."

This would have comforted Roswell more, but he was privately of the opinion that Mark was honest and would not be likely to give him any chance of detecting him in stealing. Still, by a little management in his part, he might cause him to fall under suspicion. It would of course be miserably mean on his part to implicate a little boy in a false charge, but Roswell was a mean boy, and he was not scrupulous where his dislike was concerned. He privately decided to think over this new plan for getting Mark into trouble.

"Isn't dinner ready, mother?" he asked rather impatiently.

"It will be in about ten minutes."

"I'm as hungry as a bear."

"You can always do your part at the table," said his cousin unpleasantly.

"I don't know why I should. I have to work hard enough."

"You are always talking about your hard work. My belief is that you don't earn your wages."

"I should think it was a pity if I didn't earn six dollars a week," said Roswell.

"Come, James, you're always hard on Roswell," said Mrs. Crawford. "I am sure he has hard times enough without his own relations turning against him."

James Gilbert did not reply. He was naturally of a sarcastic turn, and seeing Roswell's faults, was not inclined to spare them. He might have pointed them out, however, in a kindly manner, and then his young cousin might possibly have benefited, but Gilbert felt very little interest in Roswell.

Immediately after dinner Roswell took up his cap. His mother observed this, and inquired, "Where are you going, Roswell?"

"I'm going out to walk."

"Why don't you go with your cousin?"

James Gilbert had also taken his hat.

"He won't want to be bothered with me," said Roswell, and this statement Gilbert did not take the trouble to contradict.

"Why can't you stay in and read?"

"I haven't got anything to read. Besides I've been cooped up in the store all day, and I want to breathe a little fresh air."

There was reason in this, and his mother did not gainsay it, but still she felt that it was not quite safe for a boy to spend his evenings out in a large city, without any one to look after him.

Roswell crossed Broadway and, proceeding down Eighth Street, met a boy of about his own age in front of the Cooper Institute.

"How long have you been waiting, Ralph?" he asked.

"Not long. I only just came up."

"I couldn't get away as soon as I expected. Dinner was rather late."

"Have a cigar, Roswell?" asked Ralph.

"Yes," said Roswell, "I don't mind."

"You'll find these cigars pretty good. I paid ten cents apiece."

"I don't see how you can afford it," said Roswell. "Your cigars must cost you considerably."

"I don't always buy ten-centers. Generally I pay only five cents."

"Well, that mounts up when you smoke three or four in a day. Let me see, what wages do you get?"

"Seven dollars a week."

"That's only a dollar more than I get," said Roswell.

"I know one thing, it's miserably small," said Ralph. "We ought to get twice what we do."

"Those shopkeepers are awfully mean," said Roswell, beginning to puff away at his cigar.

"That's so."

"But still you always seem to have plenty of money. That's what puzzles me," said Roswell. "I'm always pinched. I have to pay my mother all my wages but a dollar a week. And what's a dollar?" he repeated scornfully.

"Well," said Ralph, "my board costs me all but a dollar. So we are about even there."

"Do you pay your board out of your earnings?"

"I have to. My governor won't foot the bills, so I have to."

"Still you seem to have plenty of money," persisted Roswell.

"Yes, I look out for that," said Ralph Graham significantly.

"But I don't see how you manage. I might look out all day, and I wouldn't be any better off."

"Perhaps you don't go the right way to work," said his companion taking the cigar from his mouth, and knocking off the ashes.

"Then I wish you'd tell me the right way."

"Why, the fact is," said Ralph slowly, "I make my employer pay me higher wages than he thinks he does."

93

"I don't see how you can do that," said Roswell, who didn't yet understand.

Ralph took the cigar, now nearly smoked out, from his mouth and threw it on the pavement. He bent towards Roswell and whispered something in his ear. Roswell started and turned pale.

"But," he said, "that's dishonest."

"Hush!" said Ralph, "don't speak so loud. Oughtn't employers to pay fair wages, tell me that?"

"Certainly."

"But if they don't and won't, what then?"

"I don't know."

"Well, I do. We must help ourselves, that is all."

"But," said Roswell, "what would be thought of you if it were found out?"

"There's plenty of clerks that do it. Bless you, it's expected. I heard a man say once that he expected to lose about so much by his clerks."

"But I think it would be better to pay good wages."

"So do I, only you see they won't do it."

"How much do you … do you make outside of your salary?" asked Roswell.

"From three to five dollars a week."

"I should think they'd find you out."

"I don't let them. I'm pretty careful. Well, what shall we do this evening? There's a pretty good play at Niblo's. Suppose we go there."

"I haven't money enough," said Roswell.

"Well, I'll pay for both tonight. You can pay another time."

"All right!" said Roswell though he did not know when he should have money enough to return the favor. They crossed to Broadway and walked leisurely to Niblo's Garden. The performance lasted till late, and it was after eleven when Roswell Crawford got into bed.

94

CHAPTER XVIII

THE FIRST STEP

To do Roswell Crawford justice, the idea of taking money from his employer had never occurred to him until the day when it was suggested to him by Ralph Graham. The suggestion came to him at an unfortunate time. He had always felt with a sense of bitter injustice that his services were poorly compensated and that his employer was making money out of him. Yet he knew very well that there was no chance of an advance. Besides, he really felt the need of more money to keep up appearances equal to Ralph Graham and some other not very creditable acquaintances that he had managed to pick up. So Roswell allowed Ralph's suggestion to recur to his mind with dangerous frequency. He was getting familiar with what had at first startled and shocked him.

But it was not at once that he brought his mind to the point. He was not possessed of much courage and could not help fearing that he would get himself into a scrape. It needed a little more urging on the part of Ralph.

"Well, Roswell," said Ralph a few evenings after the conversation recorded in the last chapter, "when are you going to take me to the theater?"

"I didn't know I was going to take you at all," said Roswell.

"Come, there's no use in crawling off that way. Didn't I take you to Niblo's last week?"

"Yes."

"And didn't you promise to take me some night in return?"

"I should like to do it well enough," said Roswell, "but I never have any money."

"You might have some if you chose."

"The way you mentioned?"

"Yes."

"I don't like to try it."

"Then you are foolish. It's what half the clerks do. They have to."

"So you think many do it?" said Roswell irresolutely.

"To be sure they do," said Ralph confidently.

"But I am sure it would be found out."

"Not if you're careful."

"I shouldn't know how to go about it."

"Then I'll tell you. You're in the store alone some of the time, I suppose."

"Yes, when Mr. Baker and Mr. Jones are gone to lunch."

"Where is the money kept?"

"There are two drawers. The one that has the most money is kept locked, and Mr. Baker carries away the key with him. He leaves a few dollars in another drawer, but nothing could be taken from that drawer without being missed."

"Does he keep much money in the first drawer?"

"I expect so."

"Then," said Ralph promptly, "you must manage to get into that."

"But how am I to do it?" asked Roswell. "Didn't I tell you that it was kept locked and that Mr. Baker took the key?"

"I can't say you are very smart, Roswell," said Ralph a little contemptuously.

"Tell me what you mean, then."

"What is easier than to get a key made that will fit the drawer? All you'll have to do is to take an impression of the lock with sealing wax, and carry it to a locksmith. He'll make you a key for two shillings."

"I don't know," said Roswell undecidedly. "I don't quite like to do it."

"Do just as you please," said Ralph. "Only if I carry you to the theater I expect you to return the compliment."

"Well, I'll think of it," said Roswell.

"There is another way you can do," suggested Ralph, who was full of evil suggestions and was perhaps the most dangerous counselor that Roswell could have had at this time.

"What is it?"

"If you make any sales while you are alone you might forget to put the money in the drawer."

"Yes, I might do that."

"And ten to one Baker would never suspect. Of course he doesn't know every book he has in his store or the exact amount of stationery he keeps on hand."

"No, I suppose not."

"You might begin that way. There couldn't be any danger of detection."

96

This suggestion struck Roswell more favorably than the first, as it seemed safer. Without giving a decided answer, he suffered the thought to sink into his mind and occupy his thoughts.

The next day when about the middle of the day Roswell found himself alone, a customer came in and bought a package of envelopes, paying twenty-five cents.

With a half-guilty feeling Roswell put this sum into his pocket.

"Mr. Baker will never miss a package of envelopes," he thought.

He sold two or three articles, but the money received for these he put into the drawer. He did not dare to take too much at first. Indeed, he gave a little credit to himself, so strangely had his ideas of honesty got warped, for not taking more when he might have done so.

Mr. Baker returned, and nothing was said. As might have been expected, he did not miss the small sum which Roswell had appropriated.

That evening Roswell bought a couple of cigars with the money he had stolen (we might as well call things by their right names) and treated Ralph to one.

"There's a splendid play on at Wallack's," said he suggestively.

"Perhaps we'll go tomorrow evening," said Roswell.

"That's the way to talk," said Ralph looking keenly at Roswell. "Is there anything new with you?"

"Not particularly," said Roswell coloring a little, for he did not care to own what he had done to his companion, though it was from him that he had received the advice.

The next day when Roswell was again alone a lady entered the shop.

"Have you got La Fontaine's Fables in English?" she asked. "I have asked at half a dozen stores, but I can't find it. I am afraid it is out of print."

"Yes, I believe we have it," said Roswell.

He remembered one day when he was looking for a book he wanted to read that he had come across a shop-worn copy of La Fontaine's Fables. It was on a back shelf, in an out-of-the-way place. He looked for it and found his memory had served him correctly.

"Here it is," he said handing it down.

"I am very glad to get it," said the lady. "How much will it be?"

"The regular price is a dollar and a quarter, but as this is a little shop-worn you may have it for a dollar."

"Very well."

The lady drew out a dollar bill from her purse and handed it to Roswell.

He held it in his hand till she was fairly out of the door. Then the thought came into his mind, "Why should I not keep this money? Mr. Baker would never know. Probably he has quite forgotten that such a book was in his stock."

Besides, as the price of a ticket to the family circle at Wallack's was only thirty cents, this sum would carry in him and his friend, and there would be enough left for an ice cream after they had got through.

The temptation was too much for poor Roswell. I call him poor because I pity any boy who foolishly yields to such a temptation for the sake of a temporary gratification.

Roswell put the money into his vest pocket, and shortly afterwards Mr. Baker returned to the store.

"Have you sold anything, Roswell?" he inquired on entering.

"Yes, sir. I have sold a slate, a quire of notepaper, and one of Oliver Optic's books."

Roswell showed Mr. Baker the slate on which, as required by his employer, he had kept a record of sales.

Mr. Baker made no remark but appeared to think all was right.

So the afternoon passed away without any incident worthy of mention.

In the evening Roswell met Ralph Graham, as he had got into the habit of doing.

"   Well, Roswell, I feel just like going to the theater tonight," were his first words of salutation.

"Well, we'll go," said Roswell.

"Good! You've got the money to buy tickets, then?"

"Yes," said Roswell with an air of importance. "What's the play?"

"It's a London play that's had a great run. Tom Hastings tells me it is splendid. You take me there tonight, and I'll take you to the New York Circus some evening next week."

98

This arrangement was very satisfactory to Roswell, who had never visited the circus and had a great desire to do so. At an early hour the boys went to the theater and succeeded in obtaining front seats in the family circle. Roswell managed to enjoy the play, although unpleasant thoughts of how the money was obtained by which the tickets were procured would occasionally intrude upon him. But the fascination of the stage kept them from troubling him much.

When the performance was over, he suggested an ice cream.

"With all my heart," said Ralph. "I feel warm and thirsty, and an ice cream will cool my throat."

So they adjourned to a confectionery establishment nearly opposite, and Roswell, with an air of importance, called for the creams. They sat leisurely over them, and it was nearly half past eleven when Roswell got home.

"What keeps you out so late, Roswell?" asked his mother anxiously, for she was still up.

"I was at the theater," said Roswell.

"Where did you get the money?"

"It's only thirty cents to the family circle," said Roswell carelessly. "I'm tired and will go right up to bed."

So he closed the discussion, not caring to answer many inquiries as to his evening's amusement. His outlay for tickets and for ice cream afterwards had just used up the money he had stolen, and all that he had to compensate for the loss of his integrity was a headache, occasioned by late hours and the warm and confined atmosphere at the theater.

CHAPTER XIX

RICHARD HUNTER IS PROMOTED

It was with eager importance that Mark awaited the return of Richard Hunter to communicate to him his good luck in securing a job. The thought that he had secured it by his own exertions gave him great satisfaction.

"I've got a job," were his first words as Richard entered the house.

"Already?" asked Richard Hunter. "You have been quite smart, Mark. How did you manage to obtain it?"

Mark gave the particulars, which need not be repeated.

"What kind of a store is it?"

"A bookstore."

"What is the name of your employer?"

"Baker."

"Baker's bookstore!" repeated Richard turning to Fosdick. "That is where our particular friend, Roswell Crawford, is employed."

"Yes," said Mark. "There's a boy there about sixteen or seventeen. I believe that is his name."

"I'm not sure whether his being there will make it pleasant to you. Does he know that you are a friend of mine?"

"Yes," said Mark. "He inquired particularly about you, Mr. Hunter."

"He's very fond of me," said Dick. "I suppose he sent me his love."

"No," said Mark smiling. "he didn't speak as if he loved you very much."

"He doesn't like me very much. I am afraid when he gets to be president I shan't stand much chance of an office. He didn't try to bully you, did he?"

"He said he could get me sent off if I wasn't careful to please him."

"That sounds like Roswell."

"He talked as if he was one of the firm," said Mark, "but when Mr. Baker came in, he began to scold him for not dusting the books. After that I didn't think so much of what he said."

"It's a way he has," said Fosdick. "He doesn't like me much either, as I got a job that he was trying for."

"If he bullies you, just let me know," said Richard. "Perhaps I can stop it."

"I am not afraid," said Mark. "Mr. Baker is there most of the time, and he wouldn't dare to bully me before him."

Sunday morning came, a day when the noisy streets were hushed and the hum of business was stilled. Richard Hunter and Fosdick still attended the Sunday school to which they had now belonged for over two years. They were still members of Mr. Greyson's class and were much better informed on religious matters than formerly. Frequently, for they were favorite scholars with Mr. Greyson, he invited them home to dine at his handsome residence. Both boys were now perfectly self-possessed on such occasions. They knew how to behave at the table with perfect decorum, and no one would have judged from their dress, manners, or conversation that they had not always been accustomed to the same style of living.

Mr. and Mrs. Greyson noticed with pleasure the great improvement in their protégés and always welcomed them with kind hospitality. But there was another member of the family who always looked forward with pleasure to seeing them. This was Ida, now a young lady of thirteen, who had from the first taken an especial fancy to Dick, as she always called him.

"Well, Mark," said Richard Hunter on Sunday morning, "wouldn't you like to go to Sunday school with me?"

"Yes," said Mark. "Mother always wanted me to go to Sunday school, but she was so poor that she could not dress me in suitable clothes."

"There is nothing to prevent your going now. We shall be ready in about half an hour."

At the appointed time the three set out. The distance was not great, the church being situated four blocks farther uptown on Fifth Avenue. They chanced to meet Mr. Greyson on the church steps.

"Good morning, Richard. Good morning, Henry," he said. Then, glancing at Mark, "Who is your young friend?"

"His name is Mark Manton," said Richard. "He is my ward."

"Indeed! I had not thought of you in the character of a guardian," said Mr. Greyson smiling.

"I should like to have him enter one of the younger classes," said Richard.

"Certainly, I will gladly find a place for him. Perhaps you can take him in your class."

"In my class!" repeated Richard in surprise.

"Yes, I thought I had mentioned to you that Mr. Benton was about to leave the city and is obliged to give up his class. I would like to have you take it."

"But am I qualified to be a teacher?" asked Richard, who had never before thought of being invited to take a class.

"I think you have excellent qualifications for such a position. It speaks well for you, however, that you should feel a modest hesitation on the subject."

"I think Fosdick would make a better teacher than I."

"Oh, I intend to draft him into the service also. I shall ask him to take the next vacancy."

The class assigned to our friend Dick (we are sometimes tempted to call him by his old, familiar name) consisted of boys from ten to eleven years of age. Among these Mark was placed. Although he had never before attended a Sunday school, his mother, who was an excellent woman, had given him considerable religious instruction so that he was about as well advanced as the rest of the class.

Richard easily adapted himself to the new situation in which he was placed. He illustrated the lesson in a familiar and oftentimes quaint manner so that he easily commanded the attention of the boys, who were surprised when the time came for the lesson to close.

"I am glad you are my teacher, Mr. Hunter," said one of the boys at the close of the service.

"Thank you," said Richard, who felt gratified at the compliment. "It's new business to me, but I hope I shall be able to interest you."

"Won't you come and dine with us?" said Mr. Greyson as they were leaving the church.

Richard Hunter hesitated.

"I don't know if Mark can find his way home," he said with hesitation.

"Yes, I can, Mr. Hunter," said Mark. "Don't trouble yourself about me."

"But I mean to have him too," said Mr. Greyson. "Our table is a large one, as you know, and we can accommodate three as well as two."

"Do come, Dick," said Ida Greyson.

Richard was seldom able to resist a request preferred by Ida and surrendered at discretion. So, as usual, Fosdick walked on with Mr. Greyson, this time with Mark beside him, while Richard walked with Ida.

"Who is that little boy, Dick?" asked the young lady.

"That's my ward, Miss Ida," said Richard.

"You don't mean to say you are his guardian, Dick?"

"Yes, I believe I am."

"Why," said the lively young lady, "I always thought guardians were old and cross and bald-headed."

"I don't know but that description will suit me after a while," said Dick. "My hair has been coming out lately."

"Has it, really?" said Ida, who took this seriously. "I hope you won't be bald. I don't think you would look well."

"But I might wear a wig."

"I don't like wigs," said the young lady decidedly. "If you were a lady now, you might wear a cap. How funny you'd look in a cap!" and she burst out into a peal of merry laughter.

"I think a cap would be more becoming to you," said Richard.

"Do you ever scold your ward?" asked Ida.

"No, he's a pretty good boy. He doesn't need it."

"Where did you get acquainted with him? Have you known him long?"

"He was taken sick at the door of our office one day. So I had him carried to my boarding place and took care of him till he got well."

"That was very good of you," said Ida approving. "What did he use to do?"

"He was a match boy."

"Does he sell matches now?"

"No, he has got a job in a bookstore."

"What did you say his name was?"

"Mark."

"That's a pretty good name, but I don't like it so well as Dick."

"Thank you," said Richard. "I am glad you like my name."

At this moment they were passing the Fifth Avenue Hotel. Standing on the steps were two acquaintances of ours, Roswell Crawford and Ralph Graham. They had cigars in their mouths, and there was a swaggering air about them which was not likely to prepossess any sensible person in their favor. They had not been to church but had spent the morning in sauntering about the city, finally bringing up at the Fifth Avenue Hotel where, posting themselves conspicuously on the steps, they watched the people passing by on their way from church.

Richard Hunter bowed to Roswell, as it was his rule never to be found wanting in politeness. Roswell was ill-mannered enough not to return the salutation.

"Who is that, Roswell?" asked Ralph Graham.

"It's a bootblack," said Roswell sneeringly.

"What do you mean? I am speaking of that nice looking young fellow that bowed to you just now."

"His name is Hunter. He used to be a bootblack, as I told you, but he's got up in the world, and now he's putting on airs."

"He seems to have got into good company, at any rate. He is walking with the daughter of Mr. Greyson, a rich merchant downtown."

"He's got impudence enough for anything," said Roswell, with a feeling of bitter envy which he could not conceal. "It really makes me sick to see him strutting about as if he were a gentleman's son."

"Like you," suggested Ralph slyly, for he had already been informed by Roswell, on various occasions, that he was "a gentleman's son."

"Yes," said Roswell, "I'm a gentleman's son, if I'm not so lucky as some people. Did you see that small boy in front?"

"Walking with Mr. Greyson?"

"Yes, I suppose so."

"What of him?"

"That's our errand boy."

"Is it?" asked Ralph in some surprise. "He seems to be one of the lucky kind too."

"He sold matches about streets till a few weeks ago," said Roswell spitefully.

"He sold them to some purpose it seems, for he's evidently going home to dine with Mr. Greyson."

"Mr. Greyson seems to be very fond of low company. That's all I can say."

"When you and I get to be as rich as he is, we can choose our own company."

"I hope I shall choose better than he."

"Well, let's drop them," said Ralph, who was getting tired of the subject. "I must be getting home to lunch."

"So must I."

"Come round to my room, after lunch, and we'll have another smoke."

"Yes, I'll come round. I suppose mother'll be wanting me to go to church with her, but I've got tired of going to church."

CHAPTER XX

THE MADISON CLUB

Two days afterwards, when Roswell as usual met his friend Ralph, the latter said with an air of importance, "I've got news for you, Roswell."

"What is it?" inquired Roswell.

"You've been unanimously elected a member of our club."

"Your club?"

"Yes. Didn't I ever mention it to you?"

"No."

"Well, I believe I didn't. You see I intended to propose your name as a member, and not feeling certain whether you would be elected, I thought I had better not mention it to you."

"What is the name of the club?" asked Roswell eagerly.

"The Madison Club."

"What made you call it that?"

"Why, you see, there's one fellow in the club that lives on Madison Avenue, and we thought that would be an aristocratic name, so we chose it."

Roswell liked whatever was aristocratic, and the name pleased him.

"Did you say I was unanimously elected, Ralph?" he asked.

"Yes, I proposed your name at our meeting last night. It was on account of that, that I couldn't meet you as usual. But hereafter we can go together to the meetings."

"How many fellows belong?"

"Twenty. We don't mean to have more than twenty-five. We are quite particular whom we elect."

"Of course," said Roswell in a tone of importance. "You wouldn't want a set of low fellows like that Dick Hunter."

"No. By the way, I've got your notification somewhere from the secretary. Here it is."

He drew from his pocket a note adorned with a large and elaborate seal which Roswell, opening, found read as follows:

MADISON CLUB.

MR. ROSWELL CRAWFORD.

Sir:

I have the honor of informing you that at the last regular meeting of the Madison Club you were unanimously elected a member.

Yours respectfully,

James Tracy

This document Roswell read with much satisfaction. It sounded well to say that he was a member of the Madison Club, and his unanimous election could only be regarded as a high compliment.

"I will join," he said pompously. "When is the next meeting?"

"Next Tuesday evening."

"Where does the society meet?"

"In a room on Fourth Avenue. You can come round early, and we will go together."

"All right. What do you do at the meetings?"

"Well, we smoke and tell stories and have a good time. Generally there are some snacks provided. However, you'll know all about it, when you join. Oh, by the way, there's one thing I forgot to tell you," added Ralph. "There's an initiation fee of five dollars."

"A fee of five dollars!" repeated Roswell soberly.

"Yes."

"What is it for?"

"To defray expenses, of course. There's the rent and lights and stationery and the snacks. They always, I think, have an initiation fee at clubs."

"Are there any other expenses?"

"Not much. There's only a dollar a month. That isn't much."

"I don't know how I'm going to raise five dollars," said Roswell soberly. "I could manage the dollar a month afterwards."

"Oh, you'll think of some way," said Ralph.

"My mother wouldn't give it to me, so there's no use asking her."

"Why can't you pay it out of your extra wages?" said Ralph significantly.

"I wouldn't dare to take such a large sum," said Roswell. "They would find me out."

"Not if you're careful."

"They don't keep but a few dollars in the drawer at one time."

"But didn't you tell me there was another drawer?"

"Yes, but that is always kept locked."

"Open it then."

"I have no key."

"Get one that will fit then."

"I don't like to do that."

"Well, it's nothing to me," said Ralph. "Only I should like to have you belong to the club, and you can't unless you are able to pay the initiation fee."

"I would like very much to belong," said Roswell irresolutely.

"I know you would enjoy it. We have splendid times."

"I'll see what I can do to raise the money," said Roswell.

"That's the way to talk. You'll manage to get it some way."

It was a great temptation to Roswell. The more he thought of it, the more he thought he should like to say that he was a member of the Madison Club. He had a weak love of gentility, and he was persuaded that it would improve his social standing. But he did not wish to adopt the course recommended by Ralph if there was any other way of getting the money. By the time he reached home, which was at an earlier hour than usual, he had arranged his pretext.

"I am glad you are home early," said Mrs. Crawford.

"Yes, I thought I'd come home early tonight. Mother, I wish you'd let me have four dollars."

"What for, Roswell?"

"I want to buy a new hat. This one is getting shabby."

Roswell's plan was, if he could obtain the four dollars from his mother, to make up the extra dollar out of sales unaccounted for. As to the failure to buy the hat, he could tell his mother that he had lost the money or make some other excuse. That thought did not trouble him much. But he was not destined to succeed.

"I am sorry you are dissatisfied with your hat, Roswell," said Mrs. Crawford, "for I cannot possibly spare you the money now."

"So you always say," grumbled Roswell.

"But it's true," said his mother. "I'm very short just now. The rent comes due in a few days, and I am trying hard to get together money enough to pay it."

"I thought you had money coming in from your lodgers."

"There's Mr. Bancroft who hasn't paid me for six weeks, and I'm afraid I am going to lose his rent. It's hard work for a woman to get along. Everybody takes advantage of her," said Mrs. Crawford sighing.

"Can't you possibly let me have the money by Saturday, mother?"

"No, Roswell. Perhaps in a few weeks I can. But I don't think your hat looks bad. You can go and get it pressed if you wish."

But Roswell declared that wouldn't do and left the room in an ill-humor. Instead of feeling for his mother and wishing to help her, he was intent only upon his own selfish gratifications.

So much, then, was plain -- in his efforts to raise the money for the initiation fee at the club, he could not expect help from his mother. He must rely upon other means.

Gradually Roswell came to the determination to follow the dangerous advice which had been proffered him by Ralph Graham. He could not bear to give up the project of belonging to the club and was willing to commit a dishonest act rather than forego the opportunity.

He began to think now of the manner in which he could accomplish what he had in view. The next day when noon came he went round to the locked drawer, and, lighting a piece of sealing wax which he had taken from one of the cases, he obtained a clear impression of the lock.

"I think that will do," thought Roswell.

At that moment a customer entered the store, and he hurried the stick of sealing wax into his pocket.

When the store closed, Roswell went round to a locksmith, whose sign he remembered to have seen in Third Avenue.

He entered the shop with a guilty feeling at his heart, though he had a plausible story arranged for the occasion.

"I want a key made," he said in a business-like manner, "one that will fit this lock."

Here he displayed the wax impression.

"What sort of lock is it?" asked the locksmith looking at it.

"It is a bureau drawer," said Roswell. "We have lost the key and can't open it. So I took the impression in wax. How soon can you let me have it?"

"Are you in a hurry for it?"

"Yes. Didn't I tell you we couldn't open the drawer?"

"Well, I'll try to let you have it by tomorrow night."

"That will do," said Roswell.

He left the locksmith's shop with mixed feelings of satisfaction and shame at the thought of the use to which he was intending to put the key. It was a great price he had determined to pay for the honor of belonging to the Madison Club.

CHAPTER XXI

ROSWELL JOINS THE

MADISON CLUB

It was not until Saturday night that Roswell obtained the key. The locksmith, like tradesmen and mechanics in general, kept putting him off, to Roswell's great annoyance.

As he did not get the key till Saturday night, of course there would be no opportunity of using it till Monday. The only time then was the hour in which Mr. Baker and Mr. Jones were absent, and Roswell was left alone. But to his great vexation, an old gentleman came in directly after Mr. Baker went out and inquired for him.

"He's gone to lunch," said Roswell.

"I think I'll wait till he returns," said the visitor, coolly sitting down in Mr. Baker's armchair.

Roswell was in dismay, for this would of course prevent his using the key which he had taken so much trouble to obtain.

"Mr. Baker is always out a good while," said Roswell.

"Never mind, I can wait for him. I came in from the country this morning and shall not need to start back till four."

"Perhaps," suggested Roswell, "you could go out and do the rest of your errands and come back at two o'clock. Mr. Baker will be sure to be back then."

"Who told you I had any more errands to do?" asked the old gentleman sharply.

"I thought you might have," said Roswell somewhat confused.

"You are very considerate, but, as my business is over for the day, I will ask your permission to remain till my nephew returns."

So this was Mr. Baker's uncle, a shrewd old gentleman, if he did live in the country.

"Certainly," said Roswell but not with a very good grace, adding to himself, "there'll be no chance for me to get the money today. I hope the old fellow won't come round again tomorrow."

The next day was Tuesday. In the evening the club was to meet, so there was no time to lose.

Fortunately, as Roswell thought, the coast was clear.

"Suppose the key won't fit?" he thought with uneasiness.

It would have been lucky for Roswell if the key had not fit, but it proved to fit exactly. Turning it in the lock, the drawer opened, and before him lay a pile of bills.

How much or how little there might be Roswell did not stop to examine. He knew that a customer might come in at any time, and he must do at once what he meant to do. At the top of the pile there was a five-dollar bill. He took it, slipped it hastily into his vest pocket, relocked the drawer, and, walking away from it, began to dust the books upon the counter.

He felt that he had taken the decisive step. He was supplied with the necessary money to pay the initiation fee. The question was, would Mr. Baker find out?

Suppose he should, how would it be possible to evade suspicion, or to throw it upon someone else?

"If I could make him think it was the match boy," thought Roswell, "I should be killing two birds with one stone. I must see what can be done."

The front and back of a five-dollar bill from 1863

When Mr. Baker returned, Roswell feared he would go to the drawer, but he did not seem inclined to do this.

He just entered the store and said, "Mr. Jones, I am obliged to go over to Brooklyn on a little business, and I may not be back this afternoon."

"Very well, sir," said Mr. Jones.

Roswell breathed freer after he had left the shop. It had occurred to him as possible that if the money were missed, he might be searched, in which case the key and the bill in his pocket would be enough to convict him. Now he should not see Mr. Baker again till the next day probably, when the money would be disposed of.

Mr. Baker, as he anticipated, did not return from Brooklyn before Roswell left the store.

Roswell snatched a hasty supper and went over to his friend Ralph Graham's room, immediately afterwards.

"Glad to see you, Roswell," said Ralph. "Are you coming to the club with me tonight?"

"Yes," said Roswell.

"Have you got the five dollars?"

"Yes."

"How did you manage it?"

"Oh, I contrived to get it," said Roswell, who did not like to confess in what way he had secured possession of the money.

Well, it's all right, as long as you've got it. I was afraid you wouldn't succeed."

"So was I," said Roswell. "I had hard work of it. What time do the club meetings begin?"

"At eight o'clock, but I generally go round about half an hour before. Generally, some of the fellows are there, and we can have a social chat. I guess we'll go round at half-past seven, and that will give me a chance to introduce you to some of the members before the meeting begins."

"I should like that," said Roswell.

In a short time the boys set out. They paused before a small house on Fourth Avenue and rang the bell. The summons was answered by a man.

"Any members of the club upstairs?" inquired Ralph.

"Yes, sir," said the attendant. "There's Mr. Tracy, Mr. Wilmot, and Mr. Burgess."

"Very well, I'll go up."

"Jackson," said Ralph, "this gentleman is Mr. Crawford, a new member."

"Glad to make your acquaintance, sir," said Jackson.

"Thank you," said Roswell.

"Jackson takes care of the clubroom," explained Ralph, "and is in attendance to admit the members on club nights. Now let us go upstairs."

They went up one flight of stairs and opened the door of a back room.

It was not a very imposing-looking apartment, being only about twenty square feet, the floor covered with a faded carpet, while the furniture was not particularly sumptuous. At one end of the room was a table, behind which were two armchairs.

"That is where the president and secretary sit," said Ralph.

There were already three or four youths in the room. One of them came forward and offered his hand to Ralph.

"How are you, Graham," he said.

"How are you, Tracy," returned Ralph. "This is Mr. Crawford, who was elected a member at our last meeting. Roswell, this is Mr. Tracy, our secretary."

"I am glad to see you, Mr. Crawford," said Tracy. "I hope you received the notification of your election which I sent you."

"Yes," said Roswell. "I am much obliged to you."

"I hope you intend to accept."

"It will give me great pleasure," said Roswell. "You must have very pleasant meetings."

"I hope you will find them pleasant. By the way, here is our president, Mr. Brandon. Brandon, let me introduce you to a new member of our society, Mr. Crawford."

The president, who was a tall young man of eighteen, bowed graciously to Roswell.

"Mr. Crawford," said he, "allow me, in the name of the society, to bid you welcome to our joyful and festive meetings. We are a band of good fellows, who like to meet together and have a social time. We are proud to receive you into our ranks."

"And I am very glad to belong," said Roswell, who felt highly pleased at the cordial manner in which he was received.

"You'd better go to the secretary, and enter your name in the books of the club," suggested Ralph. "You can pay him the five dollars at the same time. Here, Tracy, Mr. Crawford wants to enroll his name."

"All right," said Tracy, "walk this way if you please, Mr. Crawford."

Roswell wrote down his name, residence, and the store where he was employed.

"I see, Mr. Crawford, you are engaged in literary pursuits," said the secretary.

"Yes, for the present," said Roswell. "I don't think I shall remain long, as the book business doesn't give me scope enough, but I shall not leave at present, as it might inconvenience Mr. Baker. What is your initiation fee?"

"Five dollars."

"I happen to have the money with me, I believe," said Roswell. "Here it is."

"Thank you. That is right. I will enter you as paid. The monthly assessments are one dollar, as perhaps Graham told you."

"Yes, I think he mentioned it. It is quite reasonable, I think," said Roswell, in a tone that seemed to indicate that he was never at a loss for money.

"Yes, I think so, considering our expenses. You see we have to pay for the room; then we pay Jackson's wages, and there are cigars, etc., for the use of the members. Have you ever before belonged to a club?"

"No," said Roswell. "I have always declined hitherto (he had never before received an invitation), but I was so much pleased with what I heard of the Madison Club from my friend Graham, that I determined to join. I am glad that you are particular whom you admit as members of the club."

"Oh, yes, we are very exclusive," said Tracy. "We are not willing to admit anybody and everybody."

Meanwhile there had been numerous arrivals, until probably nearly all the members of the club were present.

"Order, gentlemen!" said the president assuming the chair and striking the table at the same time. "The club will please come to order."

There was a momentary confusion, but at length the members settled into their seats, and silence prevailed. Roswell Crawford took a seat beside Ralph Graham.

CHAPTER XXII

A CLUB NIGHT

"The secretary will read the journal of the last meeting," said President Brandon.

Tracy rose and read a brief report, which was accepted, according to form.

"Is there any business to come before the club?" inquired the president.

"I would like to nominate a friend of mine as a member of the club," said Burgess.

"What's his name?" inquired a member.

"Henry Drayton."

"Will Mr. Burgess give some account of his friend, so that the members can vote intelligently on his election?" requested Brandon.

"He's a jolly sort of fellow, and a good singer," said Burgess. "He'll help make our meetings lively. He's about my age--"

"In his second childhood," suggested Wilmot.

This produced laughs at the expense of Burgess, who took it good-naturedly.

"Has he got five dollars?" inquired another member.

"His father is a rich man," said Burgess. "There will be no fear about his not paying his assessments."

"That's the principal thing," said Wilmot. "I second the nomination."

A vote was taken which was unanimously affirmative.

"Mr. Drayton is unanimously elected a member of the Madison Club," announced the president. "Notification will be duly sent to him by the secretary. Is there any other business to come before the club?"

As there appeared to be none, Brandon added, "Then we will proceed to the more agreeable duties which have brought us hither."

He rang a small bell.

Jackson answered the summons.

"Jackson, is the punch ready?" inquired the president.

"Yes, sir," said Jackson.

"Then bring it in. I appoint Wilmot and Burgess to lend you the necessary aid."

A large flagon of hot whiskey punch was brought in and placed on the table. Glasses were produced from a closet in the corner of the room, and it was served out to the members.

"How do you like it, Roswell?" inquired Ralph Graham.

"It's -- rather strong," said Roswell coughing.

"Oh, you'll soon be used to it. The fellows will begin to be jolly after they've drunk a glass or two."

"Do they ever get tight?" whispered Roswell.

"A little lively, that's all."

The predicted effect soon followed.

Wilmot, give us a song," said Burgess.

"What will you have?" said Wilmot, whose flushed face showed that the punch had begun to affect him.

"Oh, you can give us an air from one of the operas."

"Villikens and his Dinah?" suggested Tracy.

"Very good," said Wilmot.

Wilmot was one of those who, with no voice or musical ear, are under the delusion that they are admirable singers. He executed the song in his usual style and was rewarded with vociferous applause which appeared to gratify him.

"Gentlemen," he said, laying his hand upon his heart, "I am deeply grateful for your kind appreciation of my--"

"Admirable singing," suggested Dunber.

"Of my admirable singing," repeated Wilmot gravely.

This speech was naturally followed by an outburst of laughter. Wilmot looked around him in grave surprise.

"I don't see what you fellows are laughing at," he said, "unless you're all drunk."

He sat down amid a round of applause, evidently puzzled to understand the effect of his words.

After this, David Green arose and rehearsed amid great applause a stump speech which he had heard at some minstrel entertainment which he had attended.

"How do you like it, Roswell?" again inquired Ralph Graham.

"It's splendid," said Roswell enthusiastically.

"Are you glad you joined?"

"Yes, I wouldn't have missed it for a good deal."

"I knew you'd say so. Have your glass filled. Here, Jackson, fill this gentleman's glass."

Roswell was beginning to feel a little light-headed, but the punch had excited him, and he had become in a degree reckless of consequences. So he made no opposition to the proposal but held out his glass, which was soon returned to him filled to the brim.

"Speech from the new member!" called Dunbar after a while.

"Yes, speech, speech!"

All eyes were turned towards Roswell.

"You'd better say something," said Ralph.

Roswell rose to his feet but found it necessary to hold on to his chair for support.

"Mr. President," commenced Roswell, gazing about him in a vacant way, "this is a great occasion."

"Of course it is," said Burgess.

"We are assembled tonight--"

"So we are. Bright boy!" said David Green.

"I am a gentleman's son," continued Roswell.

"What's the gentleman's name?" interrupted Wilmot.

"And I think it's a shame that I should only be paid six dollars a week for my services."

"Bring your employer here, and we'll lynch him," said Tracy. "Such mean treatment of a member of the Madison Club should meet with the severest punishment. Go ahead."

"I don't think I've got anything more to say," said Roswell. "As my head doesn't feel quite right, I'll sit down."

There was a round of applause, and Wilmot arose.

"Mr. President," he said gravely, "I have been very much impressed by the remarks of the gentleman who has just sat down. They do equal credit to his head and his heart. His reference to his salary was most touching. If you will allow me, I will pause a moment and wipe away an unbidden tear."

Here amid laughter and applause, Wilmot made an imposing demonstration with a large handkerchief. He then proceeded.

"Excuse my emotion, gentlemen. I merely arose to make the motion that the gentleman should furnish a copy of his remarks, that they may be engrossed on parchment and a copy sent to the principal libraries in Europe and America."

Roswell was hardly in a condition to understand that fun was being made of him, but listened soberly, sipping from time to time from his glass.

118

"The motion is not in order," said Brandon. "The hour for business has gone by."

The punch was now removed, and cards were produced. The remainder of the evening was spent in playing euchre and other games. Roswell took a hand but found he was too dizzy to play correctly, and for the remainder of the evening he contented himself with looking on. Small sums were staked among some of the players, and thus a taste for gambling was fostered which might hereafter lead to moral shipwreck and ruin.

This was the way in which the members of the Madison Club spent their evenings -- a very poor way, as my young readers will readily acknowledge. I heartily approve of societies organized by young people for debate and mutual improvement. They are oftentimes producers of great good. Some of our distinguished men date their first impulse to improve and advance themselves to their connection with such a society. But the Madison Club had no salutary object in view. It was adapted to inspire a taste for gambling and drinking, and the money spent by the members to sustain it was worse than wasted.

Roswell, however, who would have found nothing to interest or attract him in a Debating Society, was very favorably impressed by what he had seen of the Madison Club. He got an erroneous impression that it was likely to introduce him into the society of gentlemen, and aristocratic predilections were, as we know, one of Roswell's hobbies.

It was about eleven when the club broke up its meeting. Previous to this there was a personal difficulty between Wilmot and Tracy, which resulted in a rough-and-tumble fight in which Wilmot got the worst of it. How the quarrel arose no one could remember, the principals least of all. At last they were reconciled, and were persuaded to shake hands.

They issued into the street as a noisy throng. Roswell's head ached; the punch, to which he was not accustomed, affected him in this way. Besides this he felt a little dizzy.

"I wish you'd come home with me, Ralph," he said to his friend. "I don't feel quite right."

"Oh, you'll feel all right tomorrow. Your head will become as strong as mine after a while. I'm as cool as a cucumber."

"It's rather late, isn't it?" asked Roswell.

"Hark, there's the clock striking. I'll count the strokes. Eleven o'clock!" he said after counting. "That isn't very late."

Ralph accompanied Roswell to the door of his mother's house in Clinton Place.

"Good night, old fellow!" he said. "You'll be all right in the morning."

"Good night," said Roswell.

He crept up to bed, but his brain was excited by the punch he had drank, and it was only after tossing about for two hours that he at length sank into a troubled sleep.

CHAPTER XXIII

WHO WAS THE THIEF?

When Roswell rose the next morning he felt cross and out of sorts. His head still ached a little, and he wished he were not obliged to go to the store. But it was out of the question to remain at home, so he started out about half an hour after the usual time and of course arrived late.

"You are late this morning," said Mr. Baker. "You must be more particular about being here in good season."

Roswell muttered something about not feeling quite well.

Putting his hand into his pocket by chance, his fingers came in contact with the key which he had made to open the cash drawer. Just as he was passing Mark, he drew it out and let it drop into the side pocket of his jacket. So, if suspicions were excited, the key would be found on Mark, not on him.

The critical moment came sooner than he had anticipated.

A Mr. Gay, one of the regular customers of the bookstore, entered a few minutes later.

"Good morning Mr. Baker," he said. "Have you got a 'Tribune' this morning?"

"Yes, here is one. By the way, you are just the man I wanted to see."

"Indeed, I feel complimented."

"Wait till you hear what I am going to say. You bought a copy of 'Corinne' here on Monday?"

"Yes."

"And handed me a five-dollar bill on the Park Bank?"

"Yes."

"Well, I find the bill was a skillfully executed counterfeit."

"Indeed! I didn't examine it very closely. But I know where I took it and will give you a good bill in exchange for it."

"I locked it up lest it should get out," said Mr. Baker.

Mr. Baker and Mr. Gay conversing in the bookstore.

He went to the drawer which Roswell had opened. Roswell listened to this conversation with dismay. He realized that he was in a tight place, for it was undoubtedly the five-dollar counterfeit which he had taken and paid to the Secretary of the Madison Club. He awaited nervously the result of Mr. Baker's examination.

"Don't you find it?" asked Mr. Gay.

"It is very strange," said Mr. Baker. "I placed it at the top of a pile of bills, and now it is gone."

"Look through the pile. Perhaps your memory is at fault," said Mr. Gay.

Mr. Baker did so.

"No," he said, "the bill has disappeared."

"Do you miss anything else?"

"No. The money is just five dollars short."

"Perhaps you forgot yourself, and paid it away to a customer."

"Impossible. I always make change out of this drawer."

"Well, when you find it, I will make it right. I am in a hurry this morning."

Mr. Gay went out.

"Has any one been to this drawer?" inquired Mr. Baker abruptly.

"You always keep it locked, do you not?" said Mr. Jones.

"And keep the key myself. Yes."

"Then I don't see how it could have been opened."

"There was nothing particular about the lock. There might easily be another key to fit it."

"I hope you don't suspect me, Mr. Baker?"

"No, Mr. Jones, you have been with me for five years, and I have perfect confidence in you."

"Thank you, sir."

"I hope you don't suspect me, sir," said Roswell boldly. "I am willing to turn my pockets inside out, to show that I have no key that will fit the lock."

"Very well. You may do so."

Roswell turned his pockets inside out, but of course no key was found.

"How lucky I got rid of it!" he thought.

"Now it's your turn, Mark," he said.

"I'm perfectly willing," said Mark promptly.

He put his hand into his pocket, and, to his unutterable astonishment and dismay, drew out a key.

"I didn't know I had this in my pocket," he said startled.

"Hand my that key," said Mr. Baker sternly.

Mark handed it to him mechanically.

Mr. Baker went behind the counter and fitted the key in the lock. It proved to open the drawer with ease.

"Where did you get this key?" he asked.

"I didn't know I had it, sir," said Mark earnestly. "I hope you will believe me."

"I don't understand how you can hope anything of the kind. It seems very clear that you have been at my drawer and taken the missing money. When did you take it?"

"I have never opened the drawer, nor taken your money," said Mark in a firm voice, though his cheek was pale, and his look was troubled.

"I am sorry to say that I do not believe you," said Mr. Baker coldly. "Once more, when did you take the five dollars?"

"I did not take it at all, sir."

"Have you lent the key to any one?"

"No, sir. I did not know I had it."

"I don't know what to do in the matter," said the bookseller turning to Mr. Jones, his assistant. "It seems clear to me that the boy took the missing bill."

"I am afraid so," said Jones, who was a kind-hearted man and pitied Mark. "But I don't know when he could have had the chance. He is never left alone in the store."

"Roswell," said Mr. Baker, "have you left Mark alone in the store at any time within two or three days?"

Roswell saw the point of inquiry and determined, as a measure of safety, to add falsehood to his former offence.

"Yes, sir," he said in a apologetic tone. "I left him in the store for two or three minutes yesterday."

"Why did you leave him? Did you go out of the store?"

"Yes, sir. A friend was passing, and I went out to speak with him. I don't think I stayed more than two or three minutes."

"And Mark was alone in the store?"

"Yes, sir. I had no idea that any harm would come of it."

Mark looked intently at Roswell when he uttered this falsehood.

"You had better confess, Mark, that you took the money when Roswell was out of the store," said his employer. "If you make a full confession, I will be as lenient with you as I can, considering your youth."

"Mr. Baker," said Mark quietly, more at ease now, since he began to understand that there was a plot against him, "I cannot confess what is not true. I don't know what Roswell means by what he has just said, but I was not left alone in the store for a moment all day yesterday, nor did Roswell go out to speak to a friend while I was about."

"There seems to be a conflict of evidence here," said Mr. Baker.

"I hope the word of a gentleman's son is worth more than that of a match boy," said Roswell haughtily.

"To whom do you refer, when you speak of a match boy?"

"To HIM," said Roswell pointing to Mark. "He used to be a vagabond boy about the streets selling matches and sleeping anywhere he could. No wonder he steals."

"I never stole in my life," said Mark indignantly. "It is true that I sold matches about the streets, and I should have been doing it now, if it had not been for my meeting with kind friends."

"As to his having been a match boy, that has no bearing upon the question," said Mr. Baker. "It is the discovery of the key in his pocket that throws the gravest suspicion upon him. I must see his friends and inquire into the matter."

"Of course they will stand by him," said Roswell.

"We may get some light thrown upon his possession of the key, at any rate, and can judge for ourselves. I shall keep you employed until this matter is investigated," said Mr. Baker to Mark. "Here is a parcel of books to be carried to Twenty-Seventh Street. Come back as soon as they are delivered."

124

Mark went out with a heavy heart, for it troubled him to think he was under suspicion. Theft, too, he had always despised. He wondered if Richard Hunter would believe him guilty. He could not bear to think that so kind a friend should think so ill of him.

But Mark's vindication was not long in coming. He had been out scarcely ten minutes when Roswell, on looking up, saw to his dismay Tracy, the secretary of the Madison Club, entering the store. His heart misgave him as to the nature of the business on which he had probably come.

He went forward hastily to meet him.

"How are you, Crawford?" said Tracy.

"Pretty well. I am very busy now. I will see you after the store closes anywhere you please."

"Oh," said Tracy in a voice loud enough for Mr. Baker to hear, "It won't take a minute. The bill you gave me last night was a bad one. Of course you didn't know it."

Roswell turned red and pale and hoped Mr. Baker did not hear. But Mr. Baker had caught the words and came forward.

"Show me the bill, if you please, young gentleman," he said. "I have a good reason for asking."

"Certainly, sir," said Tracy rather surprised. "Here it is."

A moment's glance satisfied Mr. Baker that it was the missing bill.

"Did Roswell pay you this bill?" he asked.

"Yes, sir."

"For what did he owe it?"

"I am the secretary of the Madison Club, and this was paid as the entrance fee."

"I recognize the bill," said Mr. Baker. "I will take it, if you please, and you can look to him for another."

"Very well," said Tracy puzzled by the words, the motive of which he did not understand.

"Perhaps you will explain this," said Mr. Baker turning to Roswell. "It seems that you took this bill."

Roswell's confidence deserted him, and he stood pale and downcast.

"The key I presume, belonged to you."

"Yes, sir," he proclaimed with difficulty.

"And you dropped it into Mark's pocket, thus meanly trying to implicate him in a theft which you had yourself committed."

125

Roswell was silent.

"Have you taken money before?"

"I never opened the drawer but once."

"That was not my question. Make a full confession, and I will not have you arrested but shall require you to make restitution of all the sums you have stolen. I shall not include this bill, as it is now returned to my possession. Here is a piece of paper. Write down the items."

Roswell did so. They footed up little over six dollars.

Mr. Baker examined it.

"Is this all?" he said.

"Yes, sir."

"Half a week's wages are due to you, I will therefore deduct three dollars from this amount. The remainder I shall expect you to refund. I shall have no further occasion for your services."

Roswell took his cap and was about to leave the store.

"Wait a few minutes. You have tried to implicate Mark in your theft. You must wait till his return and apologize to him for what you have attempted to do."

"Must I do this?" asked Roswell ruefully.

"You must," said Mr. Baker firmly.

When Mark came in and was told how he had been cleared of suspicion, he felt very happy. Roswell made the apology dictated to him, with a very bad grace, and then was permitted to leave the store.

At home he tried to hide the circumstances attending his discharge from his mother and his cousin, but the necessity of refunding the money made that impossible.

It was only a few days afterwards that Mrs. Crawford received a letter, informing her of the death of a brother in Illinois and that he had left her a small house and farm. She had found it so hard a struggle for a livelihood in the city that she decided to remove thither, greatly to Roswell's disgust, who did not wish to be immured in the country. But his wishes could not be gratified, and, sulky and discontented, he was obliged to leave the choice society of the Madison Club and the attractions of New York for the quiet of a country town. Let us hope that, away from the influences of the city, his character may be improved and become more manly and self-reliant. It is only just to say that he was led to appropriate what did not belong to him by the desire to gratify his vanity and through the influence of a bad adviser. If he can ever forget that he is "the son of a gentleman," I shall have great hopes for him.

CHAPTER XXIV

AN EXCURSION TO FORT HAMILTON

Towards the close of May there was a general holiday, occasioned by the arrival of a distinguished stranger in the city. All the stores were to be closed, and there was to be a turnout of the military and a long procession. Among those released from duty were our three friends, Fosdick, Richard Hunter, and his ward, Mark.

"Well, Dick, what are you going to do tomorrow?" inquired Fosdick in the evening previous.

"I was expecting an invitation to ride in a barouche with the mayor," said Richard, "but probably he forgot my address and couldn't send it. On the whole I'm glad of it, being rather bashful and not used to popular enthusiasm."

"Shall you go out and see the procession?" continued Fosdick.

"No," said Dick. "I have been thinking of another plan, which I think will be pleasanter."

"What is it?"

"It's been a good while since we took an excursion. Suppose we go to Fort Hamilton tomorrow."

"I should like that," said Fosdick. "I was never there. How do we get there?"

"Cross over Fulton Ferry to Brooklyn, and there we might take the cars to Fort Hamilton. It's seven or eight miles out there."

"Why do you say 'might' take the cars?"

"Because the cars will be crowded with excursionists, and I have been thinking we might hire a carriage on the Brooklyn side and ride out there in style. It'll cost more money, but we don't often take a holiday, and we can afford it for once. What do you say, Mark?"

"Do you mean me to go?" asked Mark eagerly.

"Of course I do. Do you think your guardian would trust you to remain in the city alone?"

"I go in for your plan, Dick," said Fosdick. "What time do you want to start?"

"About half-past nine o'clock. That will give us plenty of time to go. Then, after exploring the fort, we can get lunch at the hotel and drive where we please afterwards. I suppose there is sea-bathing nearby."

Dick's idea was unanimously approved and by no one more than by Mark. Holidays had been few and far between with him, and he anticipated the excursion with the most eager delight. He was only afraid that the weather would prove unpropitious. He was up at four looking out of the window, but the skies were clear, and soon the sun came out with full radiance, dissipating the night-shadows and promising a glorious day.

Breakfast was later then usual, as people like to indulge themselves in a little longer sleep on Saturdays and holidays, but it was over by half-past eight, and within a few minutes from that time the three had taken the cars to Fulton Ferry.

In about half an hour the ferry was reached, and, passing through, the party went on board the boat. They had scarcely done so, when an exclamation of surprise was heard, proceeding from feminine lips, and Dick heard himself called by name.

"Why, Mr. Hunter, this is an unexpected pleasure. I am so glad to have met you."

Turning his head, Dick recognized Mr. and Mrs. Clifton. Both had been fellow boarders with him in Bleecker Street. The latter will be remembered by the readers of "Fame and Fortune" as Mrs. Peyton. When close upon the verge of old-maidenhood, she had been married, for the sake of a few thousand dollars which she possessed, by Mr. Clifton, a clerk on a small salary in constant pecuniary difficulties. With a portion of his wife's money he had purchased a partnership in a dry-goods store on Eighth Avenue, but with the remainder of her money Mrs. Clifton had been prudent enough to have settled upon herself.

Mrs. Clifton still wore the same ringlets and exhibited the same youthful vivacity which had characterized her when she was an inmate of Mrs. Browning's boarding house and only owned to twenty-four, though she looked full ten years older.

"How d'e do, Hunter?" drawled Mr. Clifton, upon whose arm his wife was leaning.

"Very well, thank you," said Dick. "I see Mrs. Clifton is as fascinating as ever."

"Oh you wicked flatterer!" said Mrs. Clifton, shaking her ringlets and tapping Dick on the shoulder with her fan. "And here is Mr. Fosdick too, I declare. How do you do, Mr. Fosdick?"

"Quite well, thank you, Mrs. Clifton."

"I declare I've a great mind to scold you for not coming round to see us. I should so much like to hear you sing again."

"My friend hasn't sung since your marriage, Mrs. Clifton," said Dick. "He took it very much to heart. I don't think he has forgiven Clifton yet for cutting him out."

"Mr. Hunter is speaking for himself," said Fosdick smiling. "He has sung as little as I have."

"Yes, but for another reason," said Dick. "I did not think it right to run the risk of driving away the boarders, so, out of regard to my landlady, I repressed my natural tendency to warble."

"I see you're just as bad a ever," said Mrs. Clifton in excellent spirits. "But really you must come round and see us. We are boarding in West Sixteenth Street, between Eighth and Ninth Avenues."

"If your husband will promise not to be jealous," said Dick.

"I'm not subject to that complaint," said Clifton coolly. "Got a cigar about you, Hunter?"

"No, I don't smoke."

"No, don't you though? I couldn't get along without it. It's my great comfort."

"Yes, he's always smoking," said Mrs. Clifton with some asperity. "Our rooms are so full of tobacco smoke, that I don't know but some of my friends will begin to think I smoke myself."

"A man must have some pleasure," said Clifton not appearing to be much discontented by his wife's remarks.

It may be mentioned that although Mrs. Clifton was always joyful and vivacious in company, there were times when she could display considerably ill-temper, as her husband frequently had occasion to know. Among the sources of difficulty and disagreement was that portion of Mrs. Clifton's fortune which had been settled upon herself and of which she was never willing to allow her husband the use of a single dollar. In this, however, she had some justification, as he was naturally a spendthrift, and, if placed in his hands, it would soon have melted away.

"Where are you going, Mr. Hunter?" inquired Mrs. Clifton after a pause.

"Fosdick and I have planned to take a carriage and ride to Fort Hamilton."

"Delightful!" said Mrs. Clifton. "Why can't we go too, Mr. Clifton?"

"Why, to tell the plain truth," said her husband, "I haven't got money enough with me. If you'll pay for the carriage, I'm willing to go."

Mrs. Clifton hesitated. She had money enough with her, but was not inclined to spend it. Still the prospect of making a joint excursion with Richard Hunter and Fosdick was attractive, and she inquired, "How much will it cost?"

"About five dollars probably."

"Then I think we'll go," she said, "that is, if our company would not be disagreeable to Mr. Hunter."

"On the contrary," said Dick. "We will get separate carriages, but I will invite you both to dine with us after visiting the fort."

Mr. Clifton brightened up at this and straightway became more social and cheerful.

"Mrs. Clifton," said Richard Hunter, "I believe I haven't yet introduced you to my ward."

"Is that your ward?" inquired the lady looking towards Mark. "What is his name?"

"Mark Manton."

"How do you like your guardian?" inquired Mrs. Clifton.

"Very much," said Mark smiling.

"Then I won't expose him," said Mrs. Clifton. "We used to be great friends before I married."

"Since that sad event I have never recovered my spirits," said Dick. "Mark will tell you what a poor appetite I have."

"Is that true, Mark?" asked the lady.

"I don't think it's VERY poor," said Mark with a smile.

Probably my readers will not consider that conversation very brilliant, but Mrs. Clifton was a silly woman who was fond of attention and was incapable of talking sensibly. Richard would have preferred not to have her husband or herself in the company, but, finding it inevitable, submitted to it with as good a grace as possible.

131

**Mr. and Mrs. Clifton call for a carriage to accompany
Richard, Fosdick and Mark.**

Carriages were secured at a neighboring stable, and the two parties started. The drive was found to be very pleasant, particularly the latter portion when a fresh breeze from the sea made the air delightfully cool. As they drove up beside the fort, they heard the band within playing a march, and, giving their horses in charge, they were soon exploring the interior. The view from the ramparts proved to be fine, commanding a good view of the harbor and the city of New York, nearly eight miles distant to the north.

"It is a charming view," said Mrs. Clifton with girlish enthusiasm.

"I know what will be more charming," said her husband.

"What is it?"

"A prospect of the lunch table. I feel awfully hungry."

"Mr. Clifton never thinks of anything but eating," said his wife. "I don't eat more than a little bird," said Mrs. Clifton affectedly. "I appeal to Mr. Hunter."

"If any little bird ate as much as you, he'd be sure to die of indigestion," said her husband.

"I confess the ride has given me an appetite also," said Dick. "Suppose we go round to the hotel and order lunch."

They were soon seated round a bountifully spread lunch table, to which the whole party, not excepting Mrs. Clifton, did justice. It will not be necessary or profitable to repeat the conversation which seasoned the repast, as, out of deference to Mrs. Clifton's taste, none of the party ventured any sensible remarks.

After lunch they extended their drive and then parted, as Mr. and Mrs. Clifton decided to make a call upon some friends living in the neighborhood.

About four o'clock Richard Hunter and his friends started on their return home. They had about reached the Brooklyn Broadway line, when Fosdick suddenly exclaimed, "Dick, there's a carriage overturned a little ways ahead of us. Do you see it?"

Looking in the direction indicated, Dick saw that Fosdick was correct.

"Let us hurry on," he said. "Perhaps we may be able to render some assistance."

Coming up, they found that a wheel had come off, and a gentleman of middle age was leaning against a tree with an expression of pain upon his features, while a boy of about seventeen was holding the horse.

"Frank Whitney!" exclaimed Dick.

To Frank Whitney Dick was indebted for the original impulse which led him to resolve upon gaining a respectable position in society, as will be remembered by the readers of "Ragged Dick," and for this he had always felt grateful.

"Dick!" exclaimed Frank in equal surprise. "I am really glad to see you. I am in need of a friend."

"Tell me what has happened."

"The wheel of our carriage came off, as you see, and my uncle was pitched out with considerable violence and has sprained his ankle badly. I was wondering what to do, when luckily you came up."

"Tell me how I can help you," said Dick promptly, "and I will do so."

"We are stopping at the house of a friend in Brooklyn. If you will give my uncle a seat in your carriage, for he is unable to walk, and carry him there, it will be a great favor. I will remain and attend to the horse and carriage."

"With pleasure, Frank. Are you going to remain in this neighborhood long?"

"I shall try to gain admission to the sophomore class of Columbia College this summer and shall then live in New York, where I hope to see you often. I intended to enter last year but decided for some reasons to delay a year. However, if I am admitted to advanced standing, I shall lose nothing. Give me your address, and I will call on you very soon."

"I am afraid I shall inconvenience you," said Mr. Whitney.

"Not at all," said Dick promptly. "We have plenty of room, and I shall be glad to have an opportunity of obliging one to whom I am indebted for past kindness."

Mr. Whitney was assisted into the carriage, and they resumed their drive, deviating from their course somewhat in order to leave him at the house of the friend with whom he was stopping.

"I am very glad to have met Frank again," thought Dick. "I always liked him."

CHAPTER XXV

AN IMPORTANT DISCOVERY

Mark remained in the bookstore on the same footing as before. He was not old enough to succeed to Roswell's vacant position, but Mr. Baker, as a mark of his satisfaction with him, and partly also to compensate for the temporary suspicions which he had entertained of his honesty, advanced his wages a dollar a week. He therefore now received four dollars, which yielded him no little satisfaction as it enabled him to pay a larger share of his expenses.

They were all seated in Richard Hunter's pleasant room in St. Mark's Place one evening, when Dick said suddenly, "Oh, by the way, Fosdick, I forgot to tell you that I had a letter from Mr. Bates today."

"Did you? What does he say?"

"I will read it to you."

Richard drew the letter from the envelope and read as follows:

My Dear Mr. Hunter:

I have received your letter reporting that you have as yet obtained no trace of my unfortunate grandson, John Talbot. I thank you sincerely for your kind and persistent efforts. I fear that he may have left New York, possibly in the care of persons unfit to take charge of him. It is a great source of anxiety to me lest he should suffer privation and bad treatment at this moment, when I, his grandfather, have abundance of worldly means and have it in my power to rear him handsomely. I cannot help feeling that it is a fitting punishment for the cruel harshness with which I treated his mother. Now I am amassing wealth, but I have no one to leave it to. I feel that I have small object in living. I cannot help indulging in the hope that someday, by the kind favor of Providence, he may be given back to me.

If it will not be too much trouble to you and Mr. Fosdick, I shall feel indebted to you if you will continue to watch for the lost boy. Any expenses which you may incur, as I have already assured you, will be most cheerfully paid by your obliging friend and servant,

Hiram Bates

While Richard was reading this letter, Mark listened attentively. Looking up, Richard observed this.

"Did you ever meet with a boy named John Talbot, Mark?" he inquired.

"No," said Mark, "not JOHN Talbot."

"Did you ever meet any boy named Talbot? It is not certain that the name is John."

"Talbot used to be my name," said Mark.

"Used to be your name!" exclaimed Richard in surprise. "I thought it was Manton."

"Some of the boys gave me that name because there was a story that came out in one of the story papers about Mark Manton. After a while I got to calling myself so, but my real name is Mark Talbot."

"It would be strange if he should turn out to be the right boy after all, Dick," said Fosdick. "Where is the photograph? That will soon settle the question."

Dick reading the letter from Mr. Bates.

Richard Hunter opened his desk and took out the card photograph which Mr. Bates had left with him.

"Mark," he said, "did you ever see anyone who looked like that picture?"

Mark took the picture in his hand. No sooner did his eye rest upon it than they filled with tears.

"That is my mother," he said. "Where did you get it?"

"Your mother! Are you sure?"

"Yes. I should know it anywhere, though it looks younger than she did."

"Do you know what her name was before she was married?"

"Yes, she had told me often. It was Irene Bates."

"How strange!" exclaimed Richard and Fosdick together. "Mark," continued Richard, "I think you are the very boy I had been in search of for several months. I had succeeded without knowing it."

"Please tell me all about it," said Mark. "I don't understand."

"I have a great piece of good luck to announce to you, Mark. Your grandfather is a rich man, formerly in business in New York, but now a successful merchant in Milwaukee. He has no child, no descendant except yourself. He has been anxiously seeking you, intending to give you all the advantages which his wealth can procure."

"Do you think I shall like him?" asked Mark timidly.

"Yes, I think he will be very kind to you."

"But he was not kind to my mother. Although he was rich, he let her suffer."

"He has repented for this and will try to make up to you his neglect to your mother."

Mark was still thoughtful. "If it had come sooner, my poor mother might still have been alive," he said.

"I think I had better telegraph to Mr. Bates tomorrow," said Richard. "The news will be so welcome that I don't like to keep it back a single day."

"Perhaps it will be better," said Fosdick. "You will have to give up your ward, Dick."

"Yes, but as it will be for his good, I will not object."

The next morning the following message was flashed over the wires to Milwaukee:

Hiram Bates

Your grandson is found. He is well and in my charge.

Richard Hunter.

In the course of the forenoon, the following answer was received:

Richard Hunter

How can I thank you? I will take the next train for New York.

Hiram Bates.

On the afternoon succeeding, Mr. Bates entered Richard's counting room. He clasped his hand with fervor.

"Mr. Hunter," he said, "I do not know how to thank you. Where is my boy?"

"I am just going up to the house," said Richard. "If you will accompany me, you shall soon see him."

"I am impatient to hear all the particulars," said Mr. Bates. "Remember, I know nothing as yet. I only received your telegram announcing his discovery. When did you find him?"

"That is the strangest part of it," said Richard. "I found him sick just outside the office door several weeks ago. I took him home, and when he recovered let him get a job in a bookstore; but, having become interested in him, I was unwilling to lose sight of him and still kept him with me. All this while I was searching for your grandson and had not the least idea that he was already found."

"How did you discover this at last?"

"By his recognition of his mother's photograph. It was lucky you thought of leaving it with me."

"Is his name John?"

"He says his name is Mark, but for his last name he had adopted a different one, or I should have made the discovery sooner."

"How did he make a living before you found him? Poor boy!" said Mr. Bates sighing. "I fear he must have suffered many privations."

"He was selling matches for some time -- what we call a match boy. He had suffered hardships, but I leave him to tell you his story himself."

"How does he feel about meeting me?" asked Mr. Bates.

"You are a stranger to him, and he naturally feels a little timid, but he will soon be reassured when he gets acquainted with you."

Mark had already arrived. As they entered the room, Mr. Bates said with emotion, "Is that he?"

"Yes, sir."

"Come here, Mark," he said in a tone which took away Mark's apprehension. "Do you know who I am?"

"Are you my grandfather?"

"Yes, I have come to take care of you and to see that you suffer no more poverty."

Mr. Bates stooped down and pressed a kiss upon the boy's forehead.

"I can see Irene's look in his eyes," he said. "It is all the proof I need that he is my grandchild."

It was arranged that in three days, for he had some business to transact, he should go back to Milwaukee carrying Mark with him. He went round to Mr. Baker's store the next morning with his grandson and explained to him why he should be obliged to withdraw him from his employ.

"I am sorry to lose him," said Mr. Baker. "He is quick and attentive to his duties, and has given me excellent satisfaction, but I am glad of his good fortune."

"It gives me pleasure to hear so good an account of him," said Mr. Bates. "Though he will be under no necessity of taking another job but will for several years devote himself to study, the same good qualities for which you give him credit will insure his satisfactory progress in school."

CHAPTER XXVI

CONCLUSION

It was not long before Mark felt quite at home with his grandfather. He no longer felt afraid of him but began to look forward with pleasant anticipations to his journey West and the life that was to open before him in Milwaukee. It was a relief to think that he would not now be obliged to take care of himself but would have someone both able and willing to supply his wants and provide him with a comfortable home.

He felt glad again that he was going to school. He remembered how anxious his poor mother had been that he should receive a good education, and now his grandfather had promised to send him to the best school in Milwaukee.

The next morning after their meeting, Mr. Bates took Mark to a large clothing establishment and had him fitted out with new clothes in the most liberal manner. He even bought him a silver watch, of which Mark felt very proud.

"Now, Mark," said his grandfather, "if there is any one that was kind to you when you were a poor match boy, I should like to do something to show my gratitude for their kindness. Can you think of any one?"

"Yes," said Mark. "There's Ben Gibson."

"And who is Ben Gibson?"

"He blacks boots down on Nassau Street. When I ran away from Mother Watson, who treated me so badly, he stood by me and prevented her from getting hold of me again."

"Is there any one besides?"

"Yes," said Mark after a pause. "There is Mrs. Flanagan. She lives in the same tenement house where I used to. When I was almost starved she used to give me something to eat, though she was poor herself."

"I think we will call and see her first," said Mr. Bates. "I am going to let you give her a hundred dollars."

"She will be delighted," said Mark, his eyes sparkling with joy. "It will seem a fortune to her. Let us go at once."

"Very well," said his grandfather. "Afterwards we will try to find your friend Ben."

I forgot to mention that Mr. Bates was stopping at the Fifth Avenue Hotel.

They took the University Place cars, which landed them at the junction of Barclay Street and Broadway. From thence it was but a short distance to Vandewater Street where Mark lived when first introduced to the reader.

They climbed the broken staircase and paused in front of Mrs. Flanagan's door.

Mark knocked.

Mrs. Flanagan opened the door and stared with some surprise at the visitors.

"Don't you know me, Mrs. Flanagan?" asked Mark.

"Why, surely it isn't Mark, the little match boy?" said Mrs. Flanagan amazed.

"Yes, it is. So you didn't know me?"

"And it's rale delight I am to see you lookin' so fine. And who is this gentleman?"

"He is my grandfather, Mrs. Flanagan. I'm going out West to live with him."

Mrs. Flanagan dropped a courtesy to Mr. Bates, who said, "My good woman, Mark tells me that you were kind to him when he stood in need of kindness."

"And did he say that?" said Mrs. Flanagan, her face beaming with pleasure. "Sure it was little I did for him, bein' poor myself, but that little he was heartily welcome to, and I'm delighted to think he's turned out so lucky. The old woman treated him very bad. I used to feel as if I'd like to break her old bones for her."

"Mark and I both want to thank you for your kindness to him, and he has a small gift to give you."

"Here it is," said Mark, drawing from his pocket a neat pocketbook containing a roll of bills. "You'll find a hundred dollars inside, Mrs. Flanagan," he said. "I hope they will help you."

"A hundred dollars!" cried Mrs. Flanagan hardly believing her ears. "Does this good gentleman give me a hundred dollars!"

"No, it is Mark's gift to you," said Mr. Bates.

"It's rich I am with so much money," said the good woman. "May the saints bless you both! Now I can buy some clothes for the children and have plenty left beside. This is a happy day entirely. But won't you step in and rest yourselves a bit? It's a poor room, but--"

141

"Thank you, Mrs. Flanagan," said Mr. Bates, "but we are in haste this morning. Whenever Mark comes to New York he shall come and see you."

They went downstairs, leaving Mrs. Flanagan so excited with her good fortune, that she left work and made a series of calls upon her neighbors, in which she detailed Mark's good fortune and her own.

"Now we'll go find your friend, Ben Gibson," said Mr. Bates.

"I think we'll find him on Nassau Street," said Mark.

He was right.

In walking down Nassau Street on the east side, Mr. Bates was accosted by Ben himself.

"Shine yer boots?"

"How are you, Ben?" said Mark.

Ben stared in surprise till he recognized his old companion.

"Blest if it ain't Mark," he said. "How you're gettin' on!"

"Ben, this is my grandfather," said Mark.

"Well, you're a lucky chap," said Ben enviously. "I wish I could find a rich grandfather. I don't believe I ever had a grandfather."

"How are you getting on, my lad?" inquired Mr. Bates.

"Middlin'," said Ben. "I haven't laid by a fortun' yet."

"No, I suppose not. How do you like blacking boots?"

"Well, there's other things I might like better," said Ben, "such as bein' a rich merchant, but that takes rather curious capital than blackin' boots."

"I see you are an original," said Mr. Bates smiling.

"Am I?" said Ben. "Well, I'm glad of it, though I didn't know it before. I hope it ain't anything bad."

"Mark says you treated him kindly when he lived about the street."

"It wasn't much," said Ben.

"I want to do something for you. What shall I do?"

"Well," said Ben, "I should like a new brush. This is most worn out."

"How would you like to go to Milwaukee with Mark, if I will get you a job there?"

"Do you mean it?" said Ben incredulously.

"Certainly."

"I haven't any money to pay for goin' out there."

"I will take care of that," said Mr. Bates.

"Then I'll go," said Ben, "and I'm much obliged to you. Mark, you're a brick, and so's your grandfather. I never expected to have such good luck."

"Then you must begin to make arrangements at once. Mark, here is some money. You may go with Ben, see that he takes a good bath, and then buy him some clothes. I am obliged to leave you to do it, as I must attend to some business in Wall Street. I shall expect to see you both at the Fifth Avenue Hotel at two o'clock."

At two o'clock, Mr. Bates found the two boys awaiting him. There was a great change in Ben's appearance. He had faithfully submitted to the bath and bloomed out in a tasteful suit of clothes selected by Mark. Mark had taken him besides to a barber's and had his long hair cut. So he now made quite a presentable appearance, though he felt very awkward in his new clothes.

"It don't seem natural to be clean," he confessed to Mark.

"You'll get used to it after a while," said Mark laughing.

"Maybe I will, but I miss my old clothes. They seemed more comfortable."

The next day they were to start. Ben remained at the hotel with his friend Mark feeling, it must be confessed, a curious sensation at his unusual position.

They went to make a farewell call on Richard Hunter.

"Mr. Hunter," said Mr. Bates, "money will not pay you for the service you have done me, but I shall be glad if you will accept this check."

Richard saw that it was a check for a thousand dollars.

"Thank you for your liberality, Mr. Bates," he said, "but I do not deserve it."

"Let me be the judge of that."

"I will accept it on one condition."

"Name it, Mr. Hunter."

"That you will allow me to give it to the Newsboys' Lodge, where I once found shelter and where so many poor boys are now provided for."

"I will give an equal sum to that institution," said Mr. Bates, "and I thank you for reminding me of it. As for this money, oblige me by keeping it yourself."

"Then," said Richard, "I will keep it as a charity fund, and whenever I have an opportunity of helping along a boy who is struggling upward as I once had to struggle, I will do it."

"A noble resolution, Mr. Hunter! You have found out the best use of money."

~ ~ ~

Mark is now at an excellent school in Milwaukee pursuing his studies. He is the joy and solace of his grandfather's life, hitherto sad and lonely, and is winning the commendation of his teachers by his devotion to study. A job was found for Ben Gibson where he had some advantages of education, and he is likely to do well. He has been persuaded by Mark to leave off smoking, a habit which he had formed in the streets of New York. The shrewdness which his early experiences taught him will be likely to benefit him in the business career which lies before him.

Every year Mark sends a substantial present to Mrs. Flanagan, under his grandfather's direction, and thus makes the worthy woman's life much more comfortable and easy. From time to time Mark receives a letter from Richard Hunter who has not lost interest in the little match boy who was once his ward.

So the trials of Mark the Match Boy, as far as they proceeded from poverty and privation, are at an end. He had found a comfortable and even luxurious home and a relative whose great object in life is to study his happiness.

THE END

* * *

TEACHERS GUIDE QUESTIONS FOR MARK THE MATCH BOY

1. What are three of Richard Hunter's most prevailing qualities? How have his qualities helped Henry Fosdick, Mark Manton or others? Are these important qualities to possess? Why or why not?

2. Fosdick receives a sizeable fortune in Chapter III. What is the amount he receives? How much would this amount to today?

3. In Chapter III and IV, Mr. Bates describes his doctrine. What is Mr. Bates' doctrine? Does he live up to it? Why or why not?

3a. Do you agree or disagree with his doctrine? Why or why not?

4. In Chapter IX, Mark makes a decision not to go back to Mother Watson. What prompts this decision? What would you do if you were in a similar situation as Mark?

5. Why does Richard Hunter take care of Mark in Chapter XIV? What does Richard explain to the doctor are his reasons for helping Mark? What is your opinion of Richard at this point?

6. Often the people with whom we surround ourselves can have an influence on our actions. Describe how this is true, but in different ways, for both Roswell Crawford and for Mark Manton.

7. What prevents Roswell Crawford from succeeding like Richard Hunter? Is it bad luck? What causes Roswell's "bad luck?"

8. Aside from Mark Manton, Richard Hunter and Henry Fosdick, name two other characters who are rewarded by their good deeds and qualities. What are the good deeds they do and what are the specific qualities that they possess? How do these attributes lead directly to their good fortune?

TEACHERS GUIDE ANSWERS FOR MARK THE MATCH BOY

1. Richard Hunter is studious, hard working and determined. It is with these qualities that he reaches out to Henry, Mark, Micky and others to help them in their work and studious endeavors. These qualities have helped others because Richard is able to act as a role model and teach these good habits to others.

2. Fosdick receives $2,524. In 2014, this would amount to just over $43,500.

3. Mr. Bates' doctrine is that, "We ought to help each other." Though he may not have in his younger years, Mr. Bates does live up to this doctrine: first when he pays Henry Fosdick the money he owed his father, second when he searches for his grandson in order to take care of him and third when he generously thanks each of Mark's friends and confidants.

4. Mark decides not to go back to Mother Watson after he spends his first night on his own and survives. He is also tempted by Ben Gibson's advice to leave the old woman behind.

5. Richard takes care of Mark because he feels bad for the sick, small boy. He remembers what it was like to be hard up on the street, "friendless and neglected," and he takes pity on Mark. Richard also vows to pay forward the kindness and direction he once received.

6. Roswell Crawford surrounds himself with mischievous, thieving and drunken boys and he becomes worse off for it: Roswell looses his job and cannot rely on his friends. On the other hand, Mark surrounds himself with those who are accountable and want to succeed. Mark thus follows in their footsteps.

7. Roswell Crawford's own ill intentions, actions and outlook on life prevent him from succeeding.

8. Mrs. Flanagan is kind and shows motherly affection toward Mark when he is hungry and downcast. Mr. Bates later gives Mrs. Flanagan $100 to thank her. Ben Gibson acted as a mentor and a friend to Mark, and he sticks up for Mark when Mother Watson pursues him. Ben is also rewarded: Mr. Bates buys him new clothes and offers him the chance to start a respectable life with Mark.

COMMENTARY ON "MARK THE MATCH BOY"

By Mark Irwin
A Bag of Tools

"Mark, the Match Boy: Or, Richard Hunter's Ward" (1869) is a fantastic entry point into the novels of the first great American boys' author, Horatio Alger Jr. You've probably heard the phrase "rags to riches," and maybe even heard it in the same breath as Alger's name. This is a shame, really, because while it is partially correct, it actually misses the mark of his deep and central theme, which, once discovered, will leave you with a desire to return to his work again and again.

Like every other writer who's written dozens and dozens of novels over several decades, Alger had to create a formula that would give his public what they liked about his work, but do it differently enough to keep them wanting to read his next book. One way to do that, as you know if you've read the "Harry Potter" series or Rick Riordan's "Percy Jackson" novels, is to maintain the same setting and let your characters grow up or undergo a series of adventures. And this is what Alger does here, as "Mark" is, properly speaking, the third of six books that make up the "Ragged Dick" series, which catapulted Alger to national fame.

The full title of the first volume in that series—"Ragged Dick: Or, Street Life in New York with the Boot Blacks"—is our cue for what to expect and what made his books so incredibly successful among American boys. These are books taken from real life—in Alger's case, from the life of homeless boys on the streets of New York almost 150 years ago.

The inspiration for Mark came when Alger met a tiny homeless boy who told Alger he was a "timber merchant in a small way, sellin' matches." Buying a bundle of matches at wholesale, the boy and others like him would enter office buildings and shops and attempt to sell enough to recoup their investment and make enough for food and, if possible, the night's shelter. The trouble was that having made enough for bare survival, anything left over too often slipped through their fingers and was gone the next day, leaving them once again faced with starvation.

As the subtitle of "Mark"—"Richard Hunter's Ward" (think Batman's "ward," Robin, and you'll get the idea)— implies, one of the recurring themes in Alger's novels is the idea you sometimes hear today called "pay it forward." Richard Hunter, who you know was formerly "Ragged Dick," was formerly a homeless shoeshine boy, one of the primary occupations of street boys in New York City at the time. But through the kindness and help of another, and through his own moral integrity, study and hard work, Richard begins to find his way in the world, moderately successful for a young man his way. But having been helped himself, he feels an obligation to turn and help those who were like him—in this case, Mark.

Notice that the catch here, and in all of Alger's books of boys, is that success comes not just through hard work, but hard work coupled with outside recognition and reward. In the first novel of the series, Richard (as Dick) saves the life of a young child who falls overboard off a ferry. His act of heroism leads to the child's father giving Dick a job at a counting house. You could call this an accident (as critics like Edwin P. Hoyt have done), or you could call it luck, which Alger himself did. But really, I think Alger wrote more than he knew.

Alger was the son of a minister, and what is really at work here is something of a mysterious combination of work and luck, or what the Christian tradition he grew up in called the idea of "faith and works," not just one and not just the other. It's the combination of the two that leads to the material and spiritual success of Richard Hunter and Alger's other boy heroes.

But whether it's luck, accident, hard work or all three, both Richard and Mark have hard knocks aplenty, and it's worth remarking that neither boy is ever accused by their friends of being a "goody-goody," something as repulsive 150 years ago as it is today. On more than one occasion, both boys display all-too-human weaknesses and make the kinds of mistakes that come into everyone's life.

While our world is vastly different from theirs, deep down we find some of the same basic problems: the fight against poverty, the struggle to try and make something of yourself, the need to turn away from easy entertainment and false friends. While their lives might seem strange at first glance, they certainly weren't easier. While we still have the homeless with us, what we see on our streets are mostly homeless men, not boys. Life could be very brutal for children then, much more so than today. Alger's concern was for these books to speak directly and with excitement and humor to the boys who made up his readership, and I think that shines through almost as well today as it did all those years ago.

Most of us have read, or at least know about, Mark Twain's "Tom Sawyer," probably the most famous of all American boy heroes. And I like to imagine that if Tom had picked up "Mark, the Match Boy," he would've found a good read. Tom, as you recall, was a voracious reader, especially of tales of chivalry, knights and daring-do, and like all kids both now and then, he was hard-wired to play, so when he grew up, he'd know how to work. There's a connection, you know, one that every kid who's ever played little league or dribbled a basketball down the court understands.

"Tom Sawyer, Detective" (1896), the last of Tom's adventures, came out just five years after a poem by R. L. Sharpe that expresses better than I ever could the "Bag of Tools" Alger offers the reader in "Mark, the Match Boy" and his other novels. You might even know it. It's a great way to think about what Alger was trying to accomplish in these books, so I'll leave you with it:

Isn't it strange
That princes and kings,
And clowns that caper
In saw-dust rings,
And common people
Like you and me
Are builders of eternity?
Each is given a bag of tools,
A shapeless mass,
A book of rules;
And each must make,
Ere life is flown,
A stumbling block
Or a stepping stone.

Mark Irwin received his Ph.D. in literature and religion at the University of Virginia and has spent his time since teaching the love of great books to inner-city sixth-, seventh- and eighth-graders.

THE LIFE AND THEMES OF
HORATIO ALGER, JR.

By Stefan Kanfer

The Merriam-Webster Dictionary devotes one sentence to him: "Of, relating to, or resembling the fiction of Horatio Alger in which success is achieved through self-reliance and hard work."

True as far as it goes, but that sentence reveals nothing about the man or his accomplishment. Then again, other contemporary reference books are just as terse. Not one acknowledges that Alger in his day (circa 1880-1920) was a publishing phenomenon. During those decades, when a sale of 10,000 volumes was deemed a triumph, readers bought more than 200 million copies of Alger's works, placing him in a league with J.K. Rowling and Stephen King.

Alas, today most of his novels—and there are more than 100—are out of print. But not for long. Thanks to the resuscitation efforts of Sumner Books, a division of Creators Syndicate, Alger's best literary productions are being furnished with fresh covers, new fonts and energetic promotion.

Seldom has there been a more relevant illustration of the maxim that what goes around comes around. At the turn of the 19th century, Alger was the standard-bearer of a phenomenally successful experiment in social reform and personal improvement. That movement inspired disadvantaged kids to move on up, leading juvenile delinquents into productive, significant lives. Men as different as Groucho Marx and Ernest Hemingway were fans.

"Horatio Alger's books conveyed a powerful message to me," wrote Marx, "and to many of my young friends as well—that if you worked hard at your trade, the big chance would eventually come. As a child I didn't regard it as a myth, and as an old man I think of it as the story of my life."

Hemingway's sister Marcelline recalled that during their childhood, "There was one summer when Ernest couldn't get enough of Horatio Alger." Not that Alger's boys' books influenced Papa's prose style. But there must have been something in the writer's stress on grit and self-reliance that affected young Ernest, as it did so many of his contemporaries.

By the end of the Roaring Twenties, though, Horatio Alger had become as passé as the Ford Model T. During the Depression he fared no better; Nathaniel West's satirical 1934 novel, A Cool Million, sent Alger's plots in reverse, as the naïve protagonist loses limb after limb seeking success among rapacious capitalists. Decades later, the film adaptation of Hunter Thompson's 1971 novel, Fear and Loathing in Las Vegas, presented the antihero as "Horatio Alger gone mad on drugs in Las Vegas."

What lay behind Alger's ability to enchant so many Americans—and to enrage so many others? The author's story furnishes a trove of clues:

The sickly child of a Unitarian minister in Marlborough, Massachusetts, Horatio, born in 1832, was always the smallest in his class and far from an academic star. Still, his report cards were good enough for admission to Harvard. There his academic prowess was in inverse proportion to his size (5 feet 2 inches). He won prizes, published verse and fiction in undergraduate magazines, and labeled the entire four years a period of "unmixed happiness."

Decades would pass before he found such contentment again. Upon graduation, Horatio attempted to make his way as a writer. After five unsuccessful years, he returned to Harvard, this time to study at the Divinity School. In 1860 the Reverend Horatio Alger was named minister of the First Parish Unitarian Church of Brewster on Cape Cod. Salary: $800 per year. To supplement his meager income, he turned once again to writing. This time, his stories were well-received, and he allowed himself to dream of a dual career of preacher and writer. That's when catastrophe struck.

It was of his own making, if one historian is to be believed. According to this claim, a 13-year-old told his parents that the new parson had made advances to him. An investigation began. Another lad made a similar complaint. Faced with charges of behaving inappropriately, the accused was allowed to resign—with the proviso that he leave town at once.

Sometime later, Horatio wrote a poem about one Friar Anselmo, who had committed an unspecified crime. Melancholy and remorseful, he comes across a wounded traveler and gives him aid. Whereupon an angel materializes and offers salvation:

Thy guilty stains shall be washed white again
By noble service done thy fellow man.

The fugitive repaired to New York City in the spring of 1866, resolved to live out the Christian ideal, expiating his sin by saving others. The Manhattan he entered was the epicenter of the Gilded Age, a magnet for millions of ambitious climbers, drawn by the post-Civil War boom. Out of sight of the glittering prosperity, the mansions and carriages, however, was another New York, a squalid night town that travelers compared to Calcutta, India.

In The Good Old Days, They Were Terrible, historian Otto Bettmann reports that there was scarcely a slum that pedestrians could negotiate "without climbing over a heap of trash or, in rain, wading through a bed of slime." Many streets were so dangerous that policemen hesitated to walk them alone. A Gramercy Park resident noted in his diary, "Most of my friends are investing in revolvers and carry them about at night"—and the Park was one of the city's better neighborhoods.

The New York City street urchin entered the national consciousness in those years. More than 60,000 neglected or abandoned kids ran unsupervised in the street, partly because of the fallout from the tidal waves of immigration from Europe and partly because of families broken by the Civil War.

What was to be done about these juveniles likely to die on the streets or to end up behind bars? The Reverend Charles Loring Brace founded the Children's Aid Society, designed to take homeless or abused kids away from their corrosive environments. At the same time, John Hughes, New York's first Roman Catholic archbishop, set up parochial schools and a residential institution called the Catholic Protectory, which brought up abandoned or orphaned children to be useful members of society.

Horatio Alger joined these efforts at reclamation. He, too, asked himself what could be done about homeless children. Seeking answers, he wandered through the city's worst neighborhoods. He interviewed "street arabs" who spoke of broken homes, violent confrontations with parents, doomed futures. He observed how their cocky attitudes masked a profound despair. He advised them to get real jobs instead of hanging about, squandering whatever came their way from shining shoes or picking pockets. A handful nodded in agreement, expressing the desire to change their lives; most were content to take life as they found it.

Why, he pondered, did individuals subjected to the same conditions turn out so differently? One boy might become a thief, a sociopath, even a killer. His neighbor, perhaps his brother, might aim to be an upright citizen. What was the difference between them?

What saved certain boys, he came to believe, was a quality that gave them the strength to resist sloth and temptation. In a word, character. But was this inborn? In that case determinism won the day, and change was out of the question. Or, given the right opportunity and attitude, could a dispossessed youth win his share of the American dream? The latter, Alger believed—but only if the boy stopped regarding himself as a victim.

As Alger meditated upon the worst crime of the slums—the stealing of childhood from children—an idea came to him. He would be Brother Anselmo redivivus. He had sinned against youths; now he would rescue them—and in the process save himself. As the novelist put it, by depicting the situation of city waifs, he would "excite a deeper and more widespread sympathy in the public mind, as well as exert a salutary influence upon the class of whom he is writing, by setting before them inspiring examples of what energy, ambition, and an honest purpose may achieve."

Ragged Dick became the template of the fiction to follow. Subtitled Street Life in New York with the Boot Blacks, it charted the rise of a 14-year-old boy from poverty to prosperity. Dick Hunter is an adolescent with all odds against him. He has no family, he smokes, drinks alcohol when he can afford it—not very often on the small change he gets from shining gentlemen's shoes—and sleeps on gratings in the winter.

Yet something separates him from his fellow waifs. He refuses to pick pockets like the others, won't mock his elders, and yearns to "grow up 'spectable.'" His bearing and his innate decency attract the attention of upright New Yorkers. One introduces him to his church; another presents Dick with a few dollars.

The earnest youth resolves to become literate to save his money and live a clean life. One day on a walk near South Ferry he sees a toddler fall in the water. Without hesitation, Dick jumps in and saves the drowning child. In gratitude, the father, an affluent businessman, offers the rescuer a job in his office. Gainfully employed, the onetime vagabond Dick Hunter becomes Richard Hunter Esq., and shuts the door forever on the "old vagabond life which he hoped never to resume."

Naïve? Simplistic? To the jaded, the cynical and the ignorant, yes. But not to thousands of children trapped in the real world of poverty and early death. They got the message of Ragged Dick and demanded more Horatio Alger novels with more moral lessons for them to absorb. Those books changed—and in many cases saved—lives a century before Dr. Martin Luther King Jr. stated his belief that what mattered was not the color of one's skin but the content of one's character.

Today, if you listen closely you can hear, amid the jeers, the escalating sound of the last laugh. In 1947, the Horatio Alger Association was founded. It attracts more prominent men and women now than it did then. The group is dedicated to recognizing American leaders who rose, like Alger's young heroes, from humble origins "through honesty, hard work, self-reliance and perseverance." With grants to U.S. high-school students who have "faced and overcome great obstacles in their young lives," the association encourages them to emulate such enterprising and disparate members as Oprah Winfrey and Ray Kroc, Tom Brokaw and Maya Angelou, Stan Musial and Colin Powell.

They can all testify to the truths that lie between the covers of this volume. Turn the first few pages, and you'll understand why so many followed Horatio Alger's breathless, cliff-hanging chapters leading the way from skid row to success. And why so many more are about to read that map in a world where everything has changed—except the basic truths of life.

Stefan Kanfer is an award-winning writer for City Journal and the author of numerous best-selling books.

ABOUT HORATIO ALGER, JR.

Horatio Alger was born in 1832 in Chelsea, Massachusetts. He spent his early years in the small town and under the guidance of the church and his father, the town pastor, before the family moved just west of Boston to the town of Marlborough.

As a shy young boy, Alger poured himself into books and soon became a distinguished student. He studied at Harvard and Harvard Divinity School before becoming a minister. He practiced ministry for a few years near Boston and on Cape Cod, but he was distracted by his true passion: writing.

He loved to write, and by 1865 Alger had written a handful of stories, including Frank's Campaign and Paul Prescott's Charge. The latter was the first in a series of stories that would eventually lead to his great success. In 1866, Alger moved to New York to write poetry, newspaper stories and magazine articles. However, he was shocked to find so many homeless and forgotten children among the streets, an unfortunate consequence of the Civil War. He made it his duty to aid the condition of these lost children, both through his stories and by his continuous acts of benevolence.

Horatio Alger became a household name shortly after the Civil War when he began publishing stories in the form of serializations. These serializations were featured in magazines such as Student and Schoolmate and were later compiled as books. Alger's books became enormously popular, especially among teenage boys across the country, and they soon reached millions and millions of readers. Alger continued to produce several stories a year, and, in later years, wrote novels in and of themselves instead of novels from magazine serials.

The years immediately following the Civil War were the same years when the United States emerged as one nation on the road to becoming a worldwide empire. The years between 1865 and 1900 were the years of the empire builders, with the rags-to-riches stories of John D. Rockefeller, Andrew Carnegie, Cornelius Vanderbilt and Thomas Edison. They were the years that laid the foundation for Henry Ford and other business titans and for the spectacular growth of the American economy throughout the 20th century and through today. During these years, Alger published well over 100 stories, poems and novels that spoke to the timeless themes and successes of this era.

The theme of Alger's books is consistent: If you work hard, go the extra mile, are faithful and honest, show kindness and generosity, and maintain a cheerful, positive and optimistic attitude, you will succeed in creating financial security and happiness. On the other hand, if you lie, cheat, steal, are lazy or envious, and try to take advantage of other people, you will be doomed to failure and misery. Despite his background as a preacher, Alger does not make these points in a self-righteous or pontificating way. What he does instead -- just like the parables that Jesus told -- is to create stories that illustrate the virtues that lead to success. And the stories that Alger creates are no ordinary stories. Each one is filled with lively plots and twists and turns, ones that are always unexpected and keep the reader wanting to know what's going to happen next.

As Alger grew older, he continuously strived to write the Great American Novel, little realizing that the rags-to-riches stories he created were more influential than any other novelists'. He travelled out west in early 1877 searching for new material and returned near the end of the year, producing similar stories with a new western backdrop. By 1897, Alger was suffering from asthma, bronchitis and slight short-term memory loss. He moved in with his sister in South Natick, Massachusetts where he spent the last two years of his life.

Most people have never heard of Horatio Alger while some are vaguely familiar with the term "rags-to-riches." In the Alger family, it was the norm to burn correspondence and manuscripts, and this, coupled with Alger's shyness, has greatly kept him from history's limelight. Though too often forgotten today, Alger's works and the themes within them still affect the American psyche. Many assert that there is a lagging spirit in present American culture, that these inspiring stories are irrelevant. Young people are bombarded with external stimuli that make it difficult for them to get to know themselves. Wide-eyed innocence and childlike enthusiasm, once revered as admirable qualities, are sources of mockery and disdain, which makes cynicism and pessimism inevitable. Video games, television shows, movies and music are all aimed at titillating and at seeing who can be the most gritty, violent or shocking. More than a few commentators have used the word "degrading" to describe the assault that children encounter today.

This is unfortunate. Young people need heroes and role models today just as much as they did in the 1870s and '80s, when Alger was creating them at a feverish pace from his New York City apartment, writing as many as four books at a time. Publisher A.K. Loring asserted that Alger's books "captured the spirits of reborn America" for "above all you can hear the cry of triumph of the oppressed over the oppressor ... What Alger has done is to portray the soul – the ambitious soul – of the country." Years later, biographer Edwin P. Hoyt concludes that Alger is "a writer whose influence on the American scene has been so profound that it is hard to measure." Indeed, Alger's works made an overwhelming impression on American culture and society that are still alive with us today. It is for this reason that these classics must be brought to a new generation of readers.

OUR COMMITMENT TO
HORATIO ALGER

By Rick Newcombe

Sumner Books is totally committed to reviving interest in Horatio Alger, one of the best-selling authors of all time yet someone who has been all but forgotten today. I'd like to tell you how this project came about.

Probably the best starting point is to tell you a little about myself. I grew up in suburban Chicago, and my parents were religious and fundamentally optimistic in their outlook on life. They encouraged all eight of their children to be positive in our thinking and hope and pray for the best in all situations. In my adolescence, I discovered many of the self-help authors from the 20th century, including Dale Carnegie, Napoleon Hill and Norman Vincent Peale. I remember reading a small magazine in the 1970s, when I was in my 20s, called Success Unlimited and being inspired each month to work hard and stay positive. The publisher of this magazine was W. Clement Stone, who started his career selling insurance policies door to door and who went on to build Combined Insurance, which became part of Aon, one of the largest insurance companies in the world.

By the time Mr. Stone died in 2002, he was a very successful businessman, an extremely generous philanthropist and totally committed to spreading the gospel of positive thinking. I remember reading one of his books, The Success System That Never Fails, which was both an autobiography and a blueprint for achieving success. Stone told the story of spending a summer on a farm in Michigan when he was 12, getting fresh air, helping on the farm and enjoying picnics, carnivals and camping out.

W. Clement Stone

"But I'll never forget the first day I went upstairs to the attic," he wrote, "for there I met Horatio Alger. At least 50 of his books, dusty and weather-worn, were piled in the corner. I took one down to the hammock in the front yard and started to read."

Stone said he was so enthralled he couldn't stop. "I read through all of them that summer," he wrote.

He said the principle in each book was that "the hero became a success because he was a man of character -- the villain a failure because he deceived and embezzled. How many Alger books were sold? No one knows. Estimates range from 100 million to 300 million. We do know that his books inspired thousands of American boys from poor families to strive to do the right thing because it was right and to acquire wealth."

That was the first time I had heard of Horatio Alger, but it never occurred to me to try to find his books. Over the years, I founded Creators Syndicate, which became one of the most successful newspaper syndication companies in the world. I attribute much of our success to our positive thinking and upbeat attitude. We became a multimillion-dollar international corporation by syndicating a wide variety of journalists, celebrities and award-winning cartoonists.

As we were expanding into new businesses, e-books and audiobooks were a natural starting point because we work with so many talented writers and artists. But we also wanted to try new things. With that in mind, I remembered Mr. Stone's enthusiastic recommendation of Horatio Alger's books, and I decided to read some. Many were available as e-books, and I thoroughly enjoyed them.

I had a good feeling whenever I was transported back to New York City as it was in 1870, when trains were called "cars" and there were no automobiles. There was a constant risk of crossing the streets without streetlights or walk signs. A number of years later, the Brooklyn Dodgers, now the Los Angeles Dodgers, got their name from the treacherous dodging of horses, wagons and streetcars that was required to cross the street in the city. In those days, plumbing with hot and cold running water was not taken for granted, much less radios, televisions, computers or smartphones. Are you kidding? A smartphone in the 1860s? There wasn't even a telephone.

But what great stories Alger wrote -- one after another. I couldn't get enough of them! And it was impossible not to feel grateful for all the modern conveniences of the 21st century when immersing myself in the world of America as it was in the 1860s and '70s.

As I read book after book, I felt like a teenager all over again, excited about the future and the promise of a brighter tomorrow. It was then that I decided to go full bore into spreading the word of Horatio Alger.

One of the problems with the e-books was the lack of organization; another was the maddening number of typos, over and over and over, or the lack of illustrations or the lack of a table of contents. In fact, what was intended to be a good deed to spread Mr. Alger's message really turned out to be something of a disservice.

So I made it my mission to have professional editors edit the texts so there were no typographical or spelling errors. We found appropriate illustrations. We included detailed tables of contents for each book, and we decided to publish them in groups, when appropriate, which has never been done before. We are including commentaries and teachers guides with each e-book.

We also decided to make audiobooks of as many of these "Stories of Success" as possible. We hired a terrific actor, Ben Gillman, and his initial experience shows you how far we have to go to spread the word. Ben went to the Hollywood public library to find some Horatio Alger books, but there was none. "You'd have to go to the downtown public library, in the historical section, to find those," the librarian told him.

Remember, this is one of the best-selling American authors of all time, yet it is as if he never existed.

Part of the problem is that some of the caricatures of Horatio Alger over the years have been absolutely brutal. Even to this day, the Encyclopedia Britannica, from which we expect objective reporting, calls Alger's dialogue and plots "outrageously bad." Come again? The encyclopedia is supposed to provide broad knowledge on specific subjects, not offer the biased literary criticism of a handful of editors. Talk about being unfair -- and just plain wrong!

How do you answer a cheap shot like that? Really, it is nothing more than an incredibly snooty opinion; in fact, it is an "outrageously bad" opinion. Remember, the Horatio Alger books were intended to be not great literature but rather inspirational stories to motivate young boys to achieve a better life. If the dialogue and plots were not lively and believable, the books would not have sold in the millions. The fact that Horatio Alger helped form the American character shows that an incredible number of boys ate up his books as thrilling and believable.

The brilliant writer Stefan Kanfer wrote an extensive review of Horatio Alger's works in 2000 for City Journal magazine, a publication of the prestigious Manhattan Institute. He started off believing the critics, but when he actually read some of Horatio Alger's books, he drew a totally different conclusion. "I began reading the novels aloud to my children," he wrote. "We found them well-plotted, entertaining, and instructive, not at all the righteous antiquities that I had been led to believe. Almost every chapter ends with a cliff-hanger, and all of us could hardly wait for the next night to find out what happened. The conclusions never failed to produce an emotional satisfaction and a feeling that what the author was selling -- independence, forbearance, square dealing -- was well worth buying."

We can only speculate about why the critics have been so harsh on Horatio Alger, but no doubt some it stems from their being turned off by precisely the character traits that Mr. Kanfer identifies. Like it or not, there is a mindset that scoffs at individual achievement through hard work, a positive attitude and generosity -- living every day with an "attitude of gratitude," which is the essence of Horatio Alger's message.

W. Clement Stone was routinely mocked for starting the day by saying, "I feel healthy! I feel happy! I feel terrific!" He encouraged his employees to do the same. In fact, he encouraged everyone to demonstrate outward enthusiasm and PMA, which stood for a positive mental attitude. His critics thought he was ridiculous, but Mr. Stone got the last laugh, living to age 100, which he had set as his goal, and accumulating hundreds of millions of dollars.

Roswell Crawford is an important character in Ragged Dick and Fame and Fortune because he oozes the world-owes-me-a-living attitude that is so common today. "Roswell was troubled with a large share of pride," Alger writes, "though it might have troubled himself to explain what he had to be proud of."

Roswell never understands the importance of integrity and its relationship to earning one's living. In fact, he once says that he would be happy to be paid $10 a week for nothing. "Well, if I get it, I don't care if I don't earn it," he says. In fact, Roswell is ashamed to be seen in the streets carrying a large bundle as part of a delivery for his job. Before being fired, his boss tells him, "You appear to think yourself of too great consequence to discharge properly the duties of your position."

Contrast that with Richard Hunter's attitude toward his entry-level job when he first starts working at the firm. "I'm ready to do anything that is required of me. I want to make myself useful," he says.

I have the impression that was the same attitude that Horatio Alger had as he approached his goal of becoming a successful writer who could change the world -- or at least the world of the thousands of homeless street urchins in the big city. It is difficult to imagine how bad their plight was. For instance, in 1874, which was seven years after Ragged Dick was first published, there was a little girl named Mary Ellen Wilson, who was beaten unmercifully by her stepmother. She was sent out into the streets ill-clothed in winter. There were other abuses, and they were horrible.

So a social worker named Etta Angel Wheeler wanted to intervene, to help get the child out of that environment. But there were no laws to protect children in such situations. Etta was desperate -- and clever. She enlisted the help of the American Society for the Prevention of Cruelty to Animals because animals were protected by law. Her attorneys argued that Mary Ellen, "as a member of the animal kingdom, deserved the same protection as abused animals." This led to new legislation and various child protective services.

Horatio Alger was at the forefront of this movement. He wanted to help the poor kids in the inner city, and he wound up not only helping them but inspiring millions of other young readers across the country. Many of them transformed their lives as a direct result of the inspiration of the "Stories of Success" that Horatio Alger managed to tell in one exciting setting after another.

It is not surprising that Ernest Hemingway's sister said that her brother could not get enough of Horatio Alger or that Walter Brennan, a famous actor for much of the 20th century, devoured his books. As the legendary Groucho Marx said: "Horatio Alger's books conveyed a powerful message to me and to many of my young friends -- that if you worked hard at your trade, the big chance would eventually come. As a child, I didn't regard it as a myth, and as an old man, I think of it as the story of my life."

Groucho was speaking for millions of Americans in the past and, we hope, millions more in the future.

Rick Newcombe is the founder and CEO of Creators Syndicate, Creators Publishing and Sumner Books.

PREVIEW OF ANOTHER ADVENTURE IN THE HORATIO ALGER "STORIES OF SUCCESS" SERIES

Only An Irish Boy

By Horatio Alger, Jr.

"John, saddle my horse and bring him around to the door."

The speaker was a boy of fifteen, handsomely dressed and, to judge from his air and tone, a person of considerable consequence -- in his own opinion at least. The person addressed was employed in the stable of his father, Colonel Anthony Preston, and so inferior in social condition that Master Godfrey always addressed him in imperious tones.

John looked up and answered respectfully, "Master Godfrey, your horse is sick of a disease, and your father left orders that he wasn't to go out on no account."

"It's my horse," said Godfrey. "I intend to take him out."

"Maybe it's yours, but your father paid for him."

"None of your impudence, John," answered Godfrey angrily. "Am I master, or are you, I should like to know?!"

"Neither, I'm thinking," said John with a twinkle in his eye. "It's your father who's the master."

"I'm master of the horse, anyway, so saddle him at once."

"The colonel would blame me," objected John.

"If you don't, I'll report you and get you dismissed."

"I'll take the risk, Master Godfrey," said the servant good-humoredly. "The colonel won't be so unreasonable as to send me away for obeying his own orders."

Here John was right, and Godfrey knew it, and this vexed him the more. He had an inordinate opinion of himself and his own consequence and felt humiliated at being disobeyed by a servant without being able to punish him for his audacity. This feeling was increased by the presence of a third party who was standing just outside the fence.

As this third party is our hero, I must take a separate paragraph to describe him. He was about the age of Godfrey, possibly a little shorter and stouter. He had a freckled face full of good humor but at the same time was resolute and determined. He appeared to be one who had a will of his own, but not inclined to interfere with others, though ready to stand up for his own rights. In dress he compared very unfavorably with the young aristocrat, who was biting his lips with vexation. In fact, though he is my hero, his dress was far from heroic. He had no vest, and his coat was ragged, as well as his pants. He had on a pair of shoes that were nearly double his size and fit him too largely. He wore a straw hat, for it was summer, but the brim was semi-detached and a part of his brown hair found its way through it.

Now Godfrey was just in the mood for picking a quarrel with somebody, and as there was no excuse for quarreling any further with John, he was rather glad to pitch into the young stranger.

"Who are you?" he demanded in his usual imperious tone and with a contraction of the brow.

"Only an Irish boy!" answered the other with a droll look and an Irish brogue.

"Then what business have you leaning against my fence?" again demanded Godfrey imperiously.

"Shure, I didn't know it was your fence."

"Then you know now. Quit leaning against it."

"Why should I, now? I don't hurt it, do I?"

"No matter -- I told you to go away. We don't want any beggars here."

"Shure, I don't see any," said the other boy demurely.

"What are you but a beggar?"

"Shure, I'm a gintleman of independent fortune."

"You look like it," said Godfrey disdainfully. "Where do you keep it?"

"Here!" said the Irish boy, tapping a bundle wrapped in a red cotton handkerchief, which he carried over his shoulder with a stick thrust through beneath the knot.

"What's your name?"

"Andy Burke. What's yours?"

"I don't feel under any obligation to answer your questions," said Godfrey haughtily.

"Don't you? Then what made you ask me?"

"That's different. You are only an Irish boy."

"And who are you?"

"I am the only son of Colonel Anthony Preston," returned Godfrey impressively.

"Are you, now? I thought you was a royal duke or maybe Queen Victoria's oldest boy."

"Fellow, you are becoming impertinent."

"Well, I didn't mean it. You look so proud and gintale that it's jist a mistake I made."

"You knew that we had no dukes in America," said Godfrey suspiciously.

"If we had, now, you'd be one of them," said Andy.

"Why? What makes you say so?"

"You're jist the picture of the Earl of Barleycorn's ildest son that I saw before I left Ireland."

Godfrey possessed so large a share of ridiculous pride that he felt pleased with the compliment, though he was not clear about its sincerity.

"Where do you live?" he asked with a slight lowering of his tone.

"Where do I live? Shure, I don't live anywhere now, but I'm going to live in the village. My mother came here a month ago."

"Why didn't you come with her?"

"I was workin' with a farmer, but the work gave out and I came home. Maybe I'll find work here."

"I think I know where your mother lives," said John, who had heard the conversation. "She lives up the road a mile or so, in a little house with two rooms. It's where old Jake Barlow used to live."

"Thank you, sir. I guess I'll be goin' then, as my mother'll be expectin' me. Do you know if she's well?" and a look of anxiety came over the boy's honest, good-natured face.

The question was addressed to John but of this Godfrey was not quite sure. He thought the inquiry was made of him, and his pride was touched.

"What should I know of your mother, you beggar?" he said with a sneer. "I don't associate with such low people."

"Do you mane my mother?" said Andy quickly, and he, too, looked angry and threatening.

"Yes, I do. What are you going to do about it?" demanded Godfrey.

169

"You'd better take it back," said Andy, his good-humored face now dark with passion.

"Do you think I am afraid of such a beggar as you?" sneered Godfrey. "You appear to forget that you are speaking to a gentleman."

"Shure, I didn't know it," returned Andy hotly. "You're no gentleman if you insult my mother, and if you'll come out here for a minute I'll give you a bating."

"John," said Godfrey angrily, "will you drive that beggar away?"

Now, John's sympathies were rather with Andy than with his young master. He had no great admiration for Godfrey because, during the year he had been in his father's employ, John witnessed too much of the boy's arrogance and selfishness to feel much attachment for him. Had he taken any part in the present quarrel, he would have preferred espousing the cause of the Irish boy, but this would not have been polite, and he therefore determined to preserve his neutrality.

"That ain't my business, Master Godfrey," he said. "You must fight your own battles."

"Go away from here," said Godfrey imperiously advancing toward the part of the fence against which Andy Burke was leaning.

"Will you take back what you said agin' my mother?"

"No, I won't."

"Then you're a blaggard, even if you are a rich man's son."

The blood rushed to Godfrey's face in an instant. This was a palpable insult. What! -- he, a rich man's son, the only son and heir of Colonel Anthony Preston, with his broad acres and an ample bank account -- he to be called a blackguard by a low Irish boy. His passion got the better of him, and he ran through the gate, his eyes flashing fire, bent on exterminating his impudent adversary.

BE SURE TO LISTEN TO THE AUDIOBOOK "STORIES OF SUCCESS" SERIES BY HORATIO ALGER, AVAILABLE ON AUDIBLE.COM AND ITUNES. GO TO WWW.SUMNERBOOKS.COM.

www.ingramcontent.com/pod-product-compliance
Lightning Source LLC
Chambersburg PA
CBHW060925040426
42445CB00011B/800

* 9 7 8 1 9 3 9 1 0 4 1 6 8 *